PENNINE DREAMS
the story of
THE HUDDERSFIELD
NARROW CANAL

First published 2002

PUBLISHED IN THE UNITED KINGDOM BY:
Tempus Publishing Ltd
The Mill, Brimscombe Port
Stroud, Gloucestershire GL5 2QG

PUBLISHED IN THE UNITED STATES OF AMERICA BY:
Tempus Publishing Inc.
2 Cumberland Street
Charleston, SC 29401

British Library Cataloguing in Publication Data.
A catalogue record for this book is available from the British Library.

ISBN 0 7524 2751 2

Typesetting and origination by Tempus Publishing.
Printed in Great Britain by Midway Colour Print, Wiltshire

PENNINE DREAMS
the story of
THE HUDDERSFIELD NARROW CANAL

KEITH GIBSON

TEMPUS

Acknowledgements

There are many people I must thank. Most of all the many members of the Huddersfield Canal Society and their partners in Kirklees, Oldham and Tameside Councils and British Waterways, who actively achieved restoration of the canal and gave us the story that is told here. In particular I should thank David Sumner, Trevor Ellis and all of the other members of the Huddersfield Canal Society's Council of Management for the help that they gave; David Finnis for persuading me that the canal could be restored in the first place; Geoff Brown, Bob Dewey, Chris Farrar and Derek Walker for giving me information on the early days; Frank Smith and Bob Gough in the Canal Society office for sorting out odd details that I could not easily check; Cyril Pearce who suggested where I might look for background history and information about the woollen textile industry; and Alice Lock of Tameside Local Studies Library for pointing me in the right direction on the history of the Tame Valley and the cotton industry. The map, by Bob Gough, is reproduced courtesy of Huddersfield Canal Society. Photographs and prints are individually credited. Only limited records exist of individual photographers for those reproduced courtesy of the Huddersfield Canal Society (noted as HCS), but I thank all those who wielded the cameras including David Finnis, John McLoughlin, Alan Stopher, John Sully, Stephen Whitby, Keith Sykes, Anne Wright and Ken Wright. To all of these people, I say thank you. It is not your fault if I have misunderstood or misinterpreted history. The errors and omissions are mine alone.

Keith Gibson
Holmfirth, 2002

Contents

The Huddersfield Narrow Canal

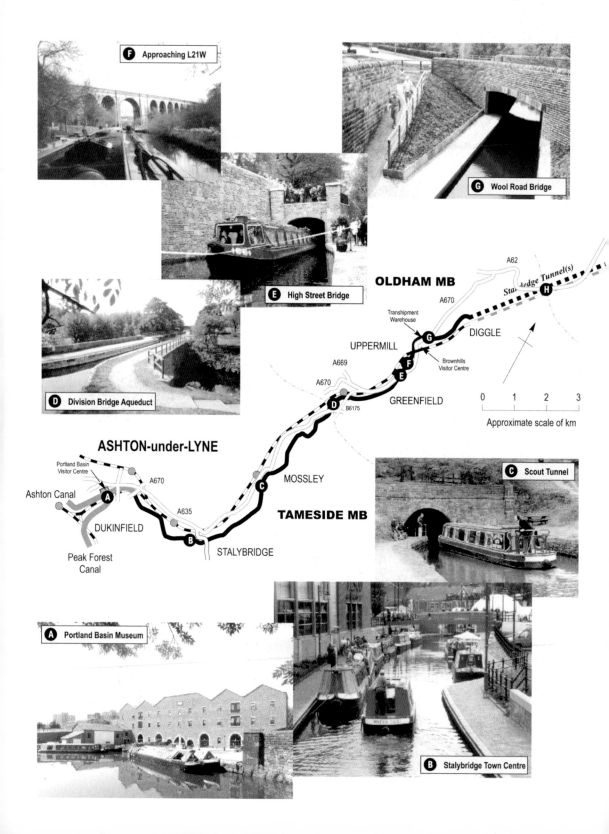

F Approaching L21W

G Wool Road Bridge

E High Street Bridge

D Division Bridge Aqueduct

OLDHAM MB

Staledge Tunnel(s)

A62

A670

DIGGLE

Transhipment Warehouse

G

UPPERMILL

A669

Brownhills Visitor Centre

F

A670

E

D

B6175

GREENFIELD

0   1   2   3

Approximate scale of km

ASHTON-under-LYNE

Portland Basin Visitor Centre

A670

Ashton Canal

A

DUKINFIELD

A635

B

C

MOSSLEY

TAMESIDE MB

C Scout Tunnel

Peak Forest Canal

STALYBRIDGE

A Portland Basin Museum

B Stalybridge Town Centre

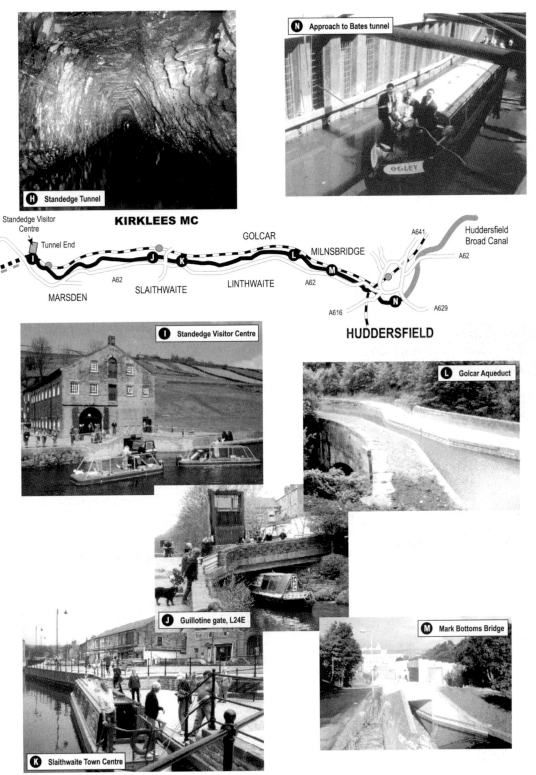

H Standedge Tunnel

N Approach to Bates tunnel

OGLEY

KIRKLEES MC

Standedge Visitor Centre

Tunnel End

GOLCAR

MILNSBRIDGE

A641

Huddersfield Broad Canal

A62

A62

SLAITHWAITE

LINTHWAITE

A62

MARSDEN

HUDDERSFIELD

A616

A629

I Standedge Visitor Centre

L Golcar Aqueduct

J Guillotine gate, L24E

M Mark Bottoms Bridge

K Slaithwaite Town Centre

Reproduced courtesy of the Huddersfield Canal Society

Boarding for a trip into Standedge, the longest, deepest and highest canal tunnel in the United Kingdom. *(Huddersfield Examiner)*

Foreword

Mikron moved to Marsden in 1978 – or, rather, my son, Sam, my wife, Sarah, and myself moved to Marsden and Mikron moved with us. We had bought a canalside cottage on the banks of the Huddersfield Narrow Canal. When we saw an advertisement for this property in *The Yorkshire Post*, we had to look up both Marsden and the canal on a map. We had never heard of either. We also had to be convinced that there really was a canal outside our back door. All we could see was a dip with many varieties of trees and shrubs flourishing in its midst. We were assured that underneath a grassy hummock lay the chamber of a lock. It wasn't long before we heard about the Huddersfield Canal Society, which had been formed in 1974. We joined more in hope than expectation that the canal would ever be fully restored to navigation. We wrote a show about the canal called *Where's Our Cut?* and toured it all over the country for two years. I spent many hours dressed as a Diggle, the mythical creatures who had lived peacefully under Standedge hill for thousands of years until disturbed by man building the Standedge Tunnel.

The public at large were still cynical, not sure that they wanted their village or town 'disrupted'. Even that doyen of the waterways, Graham Palmer, leader of the Waterway Recovery Group, said that the two canals that would definitely never be fully restored were the Rochdale Canal and the Huddersfield Narrow. The rest is history.

And it is that story which is told in this book. It is a story of perseverance and vision: the vision and almost arrogance of the late eighteenth century and early nineteenth century engineers who, with limited knowledge and very little equipment apart from manpower, believed they could build a canal underneath the Pennines, and the vision and almost blind optimism of the enthusiasts who equally believed that the canal should and could be restored along its whole length.

Keith has written an immaculately researched and detailed history of the Huddersfield Narrow Canal – the building, the commercial operation, the demise and the painstaking restoration. He has been as scrupulous in the writing of this as he has in all his years of voluntary work on behalf of the Canal Society. This book will, hopefully, stimulate and encourage many other restoration movements and demonstrate that where there's a will there's a way.

Mike Lucas
Artistic Director
Mikron Theatre Company

Introduction

This is the story of a canal. Not just any canal, but a rather special canal, the Huddersfield Narrow Canal. Twenty miles long, connecting Lancashire and Yorkshire, it has by far the longest and deepest canal tunnel built in the British Isles at Standedge under the Pennines. It was built 200 years ago by people who dreamt an impossible dream – that they might profit from a canal taking a collision course with the backbone of England; a completely inappropriate place to build a canal. Taking a long time to build, at a time when prices were rising dramatically to pay for war with France, it was thirty years before the canal company paid a dividend. The canal prospered for only a short time before a parallel railway was built, but it soldiered on in decline for another hundred years before being abandoned in 1944.

Thirty years later a group of enthusiasts dreamt another impossible dream. The world of officialdom knew that their dream of re-opening the canal was completely crazy. The canal was closed and large parts of it were destroyed. They would have to restore seventy-four locks, rebuild one and a half miles that were filled in or even built over, and reinstate bridges all along the length of the canal. It would cost millions. But the enthusiasts persevered and on 3 September 2001 the canal was officially re-opened by HRH the Prince of Wales.

So this is a story of two Pennine dreams. The first part, telling how and why the canal was built, the operating years and its decline to closure, is set in the context of what was happening in the outside world away from the canal. The second part, that of the restoration of the canal, shows how the enthusiasts achieved respectability and were taken seriously by tackling the politics of restoring the canal, raising the money, and actually doing the work. How they developed a strategy and persuaded the powers that be that the canal should be restored as a catalyst for the economic and environmental regeneration of two Pennine valleys.

1 A Pennine Dream (1)

In the spring of 1793 a public meeting was held at The George Inn in the then small Yorkshire town of Huddersfield to discuss a proposal to build a canal to Ashton-under-Lyne some twenty miles away in Lancashire. The meeting was well attended, and the plans received with much more enthusiasm than realism. The route would cross the backbone of England, the Pennines, by an enormous tunnel much longer than any proposed before, and the canal would be in competition for all but local trade with another canal following a much less severe route only a few miles to the north.

The eighteenth century was a time of change – change that became more rapid as the century drew to a close. Britain was becoming wealthy with a growing Empire. Most people lived and worked on the land, but business was thriving in the towns. Industry was expanding to supply new markets with goods. Huddersfield had become an important centre for the woollen cloth industry. Sir John Ramsden, the landowner of most of the town, built a Cloth Hall there in 1766 where clothiers and handloom weavers from the Holme and Colne Valleys to the south and west of the town, and from over the Pennines in the Saddleworth area of the Tame Valley, traded with merchants from a wide area – not just to London and the south, but to expanding markets abroad.

Developing industries and towns needed reliable and economic transport. At the beginning of the century the carrying of goods had been mainly limited to the slow packhorse. Although roads improved with the development of turnpike or toll roads, heavy carts still struggled to traverse ruts in dry weather or became stuck in the mire when it was wet. Sailing on suitable rivers and estuaries was better for bulky goods, and rivers were made navigable to bring the benefits of water transport inland. As long ago as 1699 Parliament had approved the building of lock cuts and weirs on the River Aire. Vessels could reach inland to Leeds, and the River Calder was improved from its junction with the Aire at Castleford to Wakefield. The first boats reached there in 1702. To extend navigation inland of Wakefield, the River Calder was surveyed by John Smeaton in 1757. By September 1770 the whole twenty-four miles of this, the Calder & Hebble Navigation, was open to Sowerby Bridge passing within three miles of Huddersfield at Cooper Bridge.

Across the Pennines the rivers Mersey and Irwell had been made navigable to Manchester by 1732 and in 1763, thirty years before the meeting in Huddersfield, the Duke of Bridgewater opened a canal from his coal mine at Worsley to Manchester. Although not the first canal independent of a river in the British Isles, (that being the Newry Canal in Ireland) the Bridgewater Canal was hugely influential. It proved the benefit of water transport reaching growing industrial areas away from navigable rivers. The Duke had mortgaged his estates and borrowed from his relatives and friends to build the canal, but when it reached Manchester, where extensive wharves and warehouses were soon provided at Castlefield, the price of coal fell by half overnight. The Bridgewater Canal was remarkably profitable. Other canals soon followed, beginning with the Trent & Mersey connecting the pottery districts of Stoke-on-Trent to the Rivers Trent and Mersey. James Brindley, a millwright with experience of long and complex channels feeding waterwheels, was engaged by the Duke as the engineer for his canal. The Trent & Mersey naturally appointed him too. The Trent & Mersey set a precedent for most other canals that followed, being built by a joint stock company set up for the purpose. A canal of this scale could not be financed by one man – even a wealthy man like the Duke of Bridgewater. While Brindley surveyed the Trent & Mersey he continued working on a second leg of the Bridgewater towards the Mersey, and he became much in demand from promoters of other canals. He devised a grand cross of canals connecting the Rivers Trent, Mersey, Severn and Thames. The Trent & Mersey was linked by the Staffordshire & Worcestershire Canal to the River Severn, and by the Coventry and the Oxford Canals to the River Thames. These early canals were a huge success. They revolutionised the carriage of goods and dramatically reduced the cost of commodities in the places traded to.

Soon every town worth its salt wanted a canal if it had no navigable river. And, if they could not get Brindley, other engineers filled the need. Brindley's death in 1772 did not slow the growth. Huddersfield was soon connected to the waterway network. Sir John Ramsden had died and his widow and brother controlled the estate while his son, another Sir John, was a minor. They saw that Halifax, a few miles north of Huddersfield, had benefited from the Calder & Hebble Navigation, and sought an Act of Parliament to allow the Estate to build a three-mile-long canal from Cooper Bridge to Huddersfield. The Act was approved in 1774 and Luke Holt, Surveyor to the Calder & Hebble Navigation, surveyed the route. Sir John Ramsden's Canal, built to Calder & Hebble dimensions and suitable for craft up to 57ft x 14ft (17.3m x 4.2m), was open for trade in the autumn of 1776. Wharves and warehouses were constructed at Aspley to the south of Huddersfield.

Beyond there, however, the Pennines presented a barrier to trade between Yorkshire and Lancashire. The Leeds & Liverpool Canal, approved by Parliament in 1770 to follow a roundabout route through the Aire Gap between Skipton and Colne, would do nothing for the woollen weavers of the South Pennines. It was many miles to the north and would not be complete until 1816. Brindley had surveyed a route from Manchester to Sowerby Bridge. That was not pursued for nearly thirty years until it was revived as the Rochdale Canal to link the Bridgewater Canal via Rochdale and Littleborough with the Calder & Hebble Navigation. Those early waterways had been built to accommodate barges developed from estuarial sailing craft – the Mersey Flats and Humber Keels. The Midlands canal network, however, had followed Brindley's lead on the Trent & Mersey in being built for boats of about half their beam with locks and other structures accommodating boats about 70ft (21m) long by 7ft (2.1m) wide. When John Rennie resurveyed the Rochdale Canal he proposed that it be to these smaller dimensions, limiting the cost of construction through the Pennines and the amount of water needed for lockage. But in 1792 Parliament refused consent.

What might have seemed like a branch of the proposed Rochdale Canal, the Ashton Canal, was permitted by Parliament that same year. Like Sir John Ramsden's Canal, this would improve transport to the developing textile industries of the Pennines, and it would also link coal mines between Ashton-under-Lyne and Oldham to the Manchester market. Joining the proposed Rochdale Canal at Piccadilly, Manchester, the Ashton would be a narrow canal. The main line would terminate at Dukinfield near Ashton-under-Lyne. A second Act in 1793 approved the Ashton's Hollinwood Branch and its short tributary the Fairfield Arm, to take the canal almost to the town of Oldham, and the Stockport Branch leading south to that town.

Work began on the Ashton and in 1793 a second Bill was submitted to Parliament for the Rochdale Canal. Again Parliament was not impressed and the Bill failed. In 1794 a further extension to the Ashton Canal was approved as a separate undertaking, the Peak Forest Canal. From the Ashton Canal at Portland Basin, Dukinfield, this would run south through Hyde and Marple, (where it would later be joined by the Macclesfield Canal) to Bugsworth from where a tramway would be constructed to limestone quarries at Dove Holes.

With the Rochdale Canal again failing to obtain Parliamentary approval the promoters of the Ashton Canal looked at the country between their proposed canal and Sir John Ramsden's Canal. This direct route across the Pennines, linking the valleys of the River Tame to the west and the River Colne to the east, would be by far the shortest link between the counties of

Huddersfield Cloth Hall – sadly demolished many years ago. *(Keith Gibson)*

Lancashire and Yorkshire. Local business people and, in Huddersfield Sir John Ramsden himself, were enthusiastic. A trans-Pennine canal taking local traffic and goods to and from the ports of Liverpool and Hull seemed a sure-fire winner.

Canal promotion was booming with so many schemes proposed to fill the gaps in the system in these peak years of 1792-1794 as to cause talk of a canal mania. The early canals were highly profitable. The Birmingham Canal paid as much as 17% in the 1780s. Shares in the Ashton Co. could only be bought at a premium. But the idea that large profits would be made by this, the Huddersfield Canal, was an impossible dream. Nobody told the promoters of the canal that, like the boom in dotcom internet shares of 1999 and 2000, the bubble would burst. Or that the canal would have a major problem of break of gauge with the waterways to the east and west. Or that the Pennine hills were not just something on a map. They would also be very difficult to drive a canal through. But there were pressing reasons to build a canal here.

The Pennines accounted for about one third of the value of British wool textile production. Two thirds of that output was exported to Europe and North America. The small landholdings provided a poor living from grazing sheep and farmers had diversified into handloom weaving of woollen cloth. That was now the main activity of around 500 clothiers who were selling cloth at the Huddersfield Cloth Hall. Weavers depended on yarn from carding and scribbling – separating and mixing wool to a uniform quality and fibre length – and spinning. Finishing cloth by fulling – beating it with massive wooden hammers into a strong dense pile – had long been mechanised with water-powered fulling stocks in single-storey workshops or mills. Between 1770 and 1825 spinning and carding were also mechanised. Spinning jennies were small enough to accommodate in domestic premises, but scribbling and carding engines were heavy machines. Multi-storey mills were built for them, with fulling stocks on the ground floor to provide for a growing market. The fast-flowing rivers provided power. Steam power was soon in use too. The new machines allowed the weavers to increase production and wool was imported from further and further afield especially from Lincolnshire and Leicestershire. The expanding industry desperately needed better transport to bring in bales of wool and take the finished cloth to the ports for export.

Huddersfield Market Place. The George Inn is the large building facing the viewer in this engraving by Fountain dated about 1800. *(Kirklees Cultural Services)*

A meeting was held on 17 May 1793 at an inn in the village of Marsden in the Colne Valley with John Plowes, a Leeds woollen cloth merchant who owned Whinnhill Wood Mill in the village, in the chair. It was decided to call a public meeting to seek financial backing for the canal. Advertised in the *Leeds Mercury* for 25 May, the public meeting took place five days later at The George Inn in Huddersfield Market Place when, as we have seen, the scheme was received with great enthusiasm.

An Act of Parliament would be required to authorise the line of the canal and give the company the power to compulsorily purchase land where agreement could not be reached with the landowner. Before that, however, an engineer was needed to survey the route and prepare plans. The choice of the engineer was especially important for a canal along this route. The Leeds & Liverpool was being built on a far easier route through the Aire Gap and the proposed Rochdale Canal would aim for the low pass between Littleborough and Todmorden. But there was no easy route between Ashton-under-Lyne and Huddersfield. The canal would have to cross the watershed of the Pennines at Standedge. Although the narrowest point in the South Pennine plateau and an obvious crossing point, Standedge had for long been an obstacle to travel. A Roman road passed this way between Chester and York. That remained the basis of the packhorse trail across the moor until the turnpike road was built in 1759. That was very steep and was much altered in future years to new and less steep alignments. The route of the modern A62, in use by 1839, still follows a very winding course out of the Tame Valley. It was quite a challenge for horse-drawn vehicles and the early motors. Standedge was certainly not an obvious route for a canal.

With limited capital available, early canals took indirect routes following the contours to avoid the earthworks, cuttings and embankments needed to follow a straighter line. Such a course was not possible with this trans-Pennine canal. It would involve much more adventurous engineering to traverse Standedge, and the promoters needed the best engineer they could get. James Brindley had been dead for more than twenty years. William Jessop, the leading engineer in these middle years of the canal building era, was approached. He was busy with the Grand Junction (the main line of what is now the Grand Union) and the Barnsley Canal and, perhaps more to the point, now working for the rival Rochdale scheme. Probably

The upper Colne Valley with Marsden in the distance and the canal in the centre. On the skyline the formidable obstacle of Standedge is evident, with Pule Hill prominent to the right. *(HCS)*

at Jessop's recommendation a lesser-known man, Benjamin Outram, was decided on. Only twenty-nine years old, he was assisting Jessop on the Cromford Canal in Derbyshire where his experience included a long tunnel being built at Butterley. In 1792 Outram had made a survey of the proposed Derby Canal on his own account leading to an Act of Parliament in 1793. That twelve and a half mile long canal would not be completed until 1796, however. He was also the engineer to the Nutbrook Canal linking coal mines to the Erewash Canal in Derbyshire, although the original design for that canal was Jessop's. Outram was also the founder and managing partner of a successful ironworks, Outram & Co., at Butterley on the Cromford Canal in which Jessop was a partner. Outram would no doubt be astounded to learn that in 2001 the successor to that company manufactured the steelwork for the Falkirk Wheel boat lift to take vessels between the Union and Forth & Clyde Canals in the Scottish lowlands. A few months after being appointed as engineer for the Huddersfield Canal he was also appointed as engineer for the Peak Forest Canal.

Outram presented a short written report to a second public meeting on 22 October 1793. The Huddersfield Canal would be built up the Tame Valley from Ashton-under-Lyne through or near the settlements of Stalybridge, Mossley, Greenfield, Uppermill, Dobcross and Diggle. Despite being to the west of the Pennines, the latter four settlements, with Delph and Denshaw to the north known collectively as Saddleworth, were in the West Riding of Yorkshire, and the areas in Stalybridge and Mossley to the south of the River Tame were in Cheshire. On the east the canal would climb from Huddersfield up the Colne Valley through or near the settlements of Milnsbridge, Golcar, Linthwaite, Slaithwaite and Marsden. The mass of Standedge between Diggle and Marsden would require a climb of a further 600ft, or for the canal to be taken by a three-mile-long tunnel under the hill. The Tame and Colne Valleys were steep climbs that would require the construction of many locks, but the real problem to be overcome was the sheer magnitude of this tunnel that, from the start, was recognised as being the only realistic option at Standedge. Nothing of this scale had been attempted before.

Basing his plans on a survey carried out by a Saddleworth man, Nicholas Brown, Outram recommended the canal be built as a narrow canal like the Ashton and the proposed Rochdale

Canals. He estimated the cost of the canal and feeder reservoirs at £178,748. It is easy to be misled by this apparent precision. It was the sum of a series of generalised rates for the job such as the rate of £70 per foot (305mm) rise that he allowed for locks in the Tame Valley. Outram had not been paid to prepare detailed plans, and no discussions had begun with landowners to establish land costs or the need for accommodation bridges connecting land divided by the canal. He had done enough work, however, to conclude that:

> *The line…described is in every respect practicable, and forms the shortest communication yet pointed out between Manchester and the Eastern Navigations; it will pass through a country full of manufactures which at present are carried out under great disadvantages.*

Despite Outram's optimism, a Trans-Pennine canal taking a collision course with the Pennines at Standedge would prove beyond the bounds of economic reality. But the subscribers to the scheme pressed on with a submission to Parliament and dreamt their impossible dreams of profit. Optimism was such that £150,000 of the £200,000 in £100 shares in the company required to build the canal had been committed as soon as shares were offered, although subscribers only had to put down £1 per share at the outset with the remainder to be subscribed as the company needed the money to build the canal. To be fair, many were not just subscribing to the canal to profit directly from it. The improved communications offered by the canal would be a huge boost to the communities through which it would pass: communities in which their businesses were located.

Outram and Brown prepared the information required under Parliamentary Standing Orders: a plan of the canal, details of land ownership, an approximate bill of quantities and an estimate of the cost. The plans were simple; detailed design of such matters as the number and siting of locks would be resolved later. The size of the reservoirs to feed the canal had been increased since the public meeting to assuage the fears of mill owners that the canal would take their water, and the estimated cost increased to £182,748. The major work, the building of the great tunnel at Standedge, was thought likely to take five years at a cost of £55,187.

Unlike the rival Rochdale scheme, the Bill for the canal had an easy passage through Parliament. There was yet no competing waterway to object, the owners of the water-powered mills were satisfied with the provision of reservoirs for water supply and major landowners had no objections. On 4 April 1794 the Act authorising construction of the Huddersfield Canal received the assent of Parliament.

2 Building the Canal

With Parliamentary approval gained the Huddersfield Canal Co. was formally established. A Committee of twenty business people (weavers, farmers and gentlemen) was elected to manage the company – the Board of Directors in modern terms. Local clothiers, woolstaplers, cloth dressers and other small traders were the main investors. They were interested in improved transport for their own businesses rather than in profits from the canal, but if profits were made they would not object. Indeed expected profit was the motive of some investors. Shares in the company that had been purchased for £1 changed hands for as much as £15.

George Worthington, a solicitor from Altrincham in Cheshire, was appointed as Clerk to the Company – a role he also performed for the Ashton and Peak Forest Canal Companies – and Benjamin Outram was confirmed as engineer. He was a consultant rather than an employee. He had other interests and other clients. He would provide designs and specifications of work and occasionally inspect the work. The company paid him three guineas a day while working on the canal with ten guineas expenses for each journey to the canal. They hoped to see him on site for four or five days each month and to attend meetings of the Committee.

The resident engineer was the man who controlled the building of a canal, a hard task here taking into account the physical length of the project and the difficulty of travel in the Pennines. Not only would he spend many hours on horseback, likely as not in pouring rain or worse but, alighting, he would have to deal with contractors building the canal. They were paid for the amount of work carried out, but paid their workers by the day or the hour. They were naturally concerned more with quantity than quality. The quicker they completed a task, the sooner would they be paid and the greater the profit. The poor resident engineer's interests were with both quantity and quality. He needed to keep the work rate up; the sooner the canal was built the sooner would tolls generate an income, but he also needed to ensure that the canal was properly built. The company appointed Nicholas Brown, who had carried out the initial survey for Outram, to this role at a salary of £315. He had to find his own expenses and pay a bookkeeper and any assistants he might need.

It was a bad time to be building a canal, however. The American colonies had been lost ten years earlier and in 1793 the French, in the midst of their Revolution, had invaded the Low Countries bringing Britain into a war with France to defend her allies. The 40,000 men in the army in 1789 rose to half a million in this period. Inflation resulted from the cost and economic disruption of the war, and a series of bad harvests increased the price of food. Even worse for the woollen weavers and clothiers of these Pennine valleys, crucial export markets were closed by blockades of the ports by both sides in the war. Trying to keep their businesses going with rising costs and trade hard to come by, they were hit even harder by ever increasing taxes to pay for the war. It was an even worse time to be building this particular canal. Parliament approved the Rochdale Canal on the very same day as the Huddersfield Canal. The Rochdale promoters had submitted a new plan for a narrow canal by William Jessop. Although Parliament was more amenable, this time there was a cost. The Parliamentary Committee that considered the Bill required the canal to be built as a broad waterway with locks long enough to take the narrow boats of the Midlands and wide enough to take the barges of the Calder & Hebble Navigation and the Bridgewater Canal that it would join.

Work had started on building the Ashton Canal as a narrow canal and the Ashton Company showed no great anxiety to re-think the scale of their canal to match the Rochdale, so there was no occasion to reconsider the scale of the Huddersfield. That was just as well. The company would have struggled to raise extra money for broad locks, bridges and a larger diameter tunnel, and lacked the leadership of a dominant personality to embark on that task. Changes of Chairman from meeting to meeting would characterise the annual General Assembly of Proprietors of the Company and, worse, the regular meetings of the Committee. The first General Assembly of Proprietors, when the Committee was elected, had so much business that it extended over three days, with a different Chairman each day – William Walker, John Plowes and the Revd John Lowe.

Work began, with the company immediately penny-pinching in the support needed to Nicholas Brown, especially as he had never been a resident engineer or built a canal before. He needed assistants to deal with engineering work of this complexity, but he was unwilling to pay them from his own income. The company appointed overlookers, but they were unqualified and not really up to the job. Brown was instructed to concentrate on opening the extremities of the canal to get income from trade to Slaithwaite in the east and Stalybridge in the west, but the circumstances of the war made things difficult. Prices had risen since Outram estimated the cost in 1793. Many shareholders stretched by the unpropitious times were far from happy to pay up on calls on their shares for the money needed to build the canal. The Clerk was instructed to take legal action against some of them as early as 1 January 1795.

By 1796 the Ashton Canal was open from Ancoats near Manchester to the junction with the Huddersfield Canal, but the war was going badly. Britain was threatened with invasion. General commodity prices were at least 20% higher than when Outram estimated the cost of the canal. £20,000 of the estimate of £55,000 for Standedge Tunnel had already been spent, with heavy costs of pumping water from the workings, but Outram reported to the General Assembly of Proprietors of the Company in June that he had no reason to think the original estimate of costs would be wrong. Possibly he hoped inflation would be a temporary phenomenon and he could find savings later. The company had only £889 in the bank. Of the £92,000 demanded from shareholders, £22,652 was unpaid.

The canal was open between Ashton-under-Lyne and Stalybridge in November 1796, and the longer length from Huddersfield to Slaithwaite in March 1797. The following month the company was overdrawn on its account. The Committee panicked and ordered work to stop. Only when Outram pointed out the futility of this did they find another means of raising money by arranging a mortgage on their existing property. Later in 1797 the length from Stalybridge to Mossley was open. With parts of the canal open trade could be attracted. The tolls paid would help with the cost of construction.

Nicholas Brown was inexperienced and over-worked. There was evidence of poor supervision, bad workmanship and errors in setting out. Claims for damages and trespass were not properly investigated and substantial sums were paid in compensation. A competent resident engineer would have stamped on poor work or fraudulent claims, but the Huddersfield Canal Co. was not alone in having an over-worked and ineffectual resident engineer. Many canal companies had similar difficulties. So concerned was the Committee that they decided to inspect accommodation bridges and other works themselves. I doubt that they acted on that. In July 1797, as Brown could not cope, the company appointed William Bailiffe of Marsden to take charge of construction west of Standedge, leaving Brown to concentrate on the Colne Valley and Standedge Tunnel. Then an unnecessary culvert was built and Brown was given six months notice to quit. The company changed its mind, however, and in February 1798 extended his contract for another twelve months, but at half of his previous pay. William Bailiffe was to be paid £125 per annum.

Outram had been ill and unable to give the canal the attention it needed, but he must still have been offended when in 1797 the Committee instructed Robert Whitworth, who had learnt his trade as an assistant to Brindley but was now engineer to the Forth & Clyde and the

Leeds & Liverpool Canals, to inspect the work. Whitworth's report described the works as he found them. On the west side work was well advanced to Uppermill, but little work had been done beyond there to Standedge. On the east side work was going on cutting the canal between Slaithwaite and Marsden and a bridge was being built over the canal at Slaithwaite. He thought the masonry of the locks here was better than in Ashton but several pounds between locks were dry or below the intended water level because the clay puddle waterproofing of the canal bed was inadequate.

Whitworth was 'really alarmed...to see how little [was] done' at Standedge, which he acknowledged was 'the most stupendous piece of work of the kind that has ever been projected in the Kingdom.' Canal tunnels owed much to mining practice. A line was pegged out normally using surveying poles aligned in as straight a line as possible by eye over the hill. At regular intervals vertical construction shafts were dug to the required depth below the hill. The alignment on the ground was transcribed to the bottom of these shafts. The bore of the tunnel was then excavated from the two ends and from the bottom of the shafts. The workings from the various faces would meet up to create the complete bore of the tunnel. Fine in theory, but far from foolproof in practice. It was difficult with the techniques and resources available to ensure the line pegged out was actually straight and to accurately transcribe that line to the bottom of construction shafts. It was equally difficult to ensure that shafts were dug to exactly the right depth or that the tunnel entrances at opposite ends of the hill were at exactly the same level. These problems were especially severe at Standedge because of the length of the tunnel, its depth underground and the steepness of the hill.

Whitworth found the tunnel excavated for about 500 yards (457m) at the Diggle end and 700 yards (640m) at the Marsden end, partly by driving the bore from the mouths of the tunnel and partly from shallow vertical shafts. Excavation of the central part had not begun. The construction shafts had not yet reached the level of the tunnel. The deepest, the 160 yard (146m) Engine Pit at Red Brook, was almost 80% complete but none of the other deep shafts reached even half way and one was abandoned; it flooded faster than pumps could clear. It would take a long time to dig shafts to this depth with simple tools and gunpowder, but that had been compounded by problems draining the shafts and the stop/start nature of work as the company tried to control its precarious finances. The Committee insisted on working as many shafts as possible. That meant more working faces and the possibility of completing the tunnel sooner. Outram had recommended this but he soon told the company that with a tunnel at this depth, and to limit expenditure, it would be better to concentrate on driving the tunnel from the ends and only excavate one vertical shaft to complete the central section. His advice was ignored. The huge effort put into digging the shafts meant that progress on the tunnel itself was limited. Whitworth pointed out the folly of saving money by using inadequate pumps to keep the workings clear of water. Steam pumps had been in use, but when larger pumps were required they had been more expensive than the company could afford.

On reading this, the committee must have resorted to a sharp collective intake of breath. Faced with the stark reality of very little progress in building the huge tunnel they did, perhaps, all that they were able to do at the time – prevaricate. The war with France was not going well, taxes were rising and the Bank of England had abandoned the Gold Standard as a measure of the value of banknotes. The trade of the woollen weavers and clothiers had improved since 1794, but the company was still having difficulty obtaining money owed by shareholders hard-pressed by wartime conditions. There was some good news, however. The canal was open from Slaithwaite to Marsden in 1798 and the short length of the Ashton Canal from Ancoats to Piccadilly was completed that year, although it was not until 1800 that the Rochdale Company managed to connect to the Ashton and open the nine locks between the junction and the Bridgewater Canal at Castlefield. Benjamin Outram had been appointed as engineer to the Ashton Canal in August 1798 (that company having muddled along with local surveyors William Bennet and James Meadows) and he had been the contractor for the canal between Ancoats and Piccadilly.

The short length of canal from Uppermill to Wool Road, Dobcross came into use in 1799. That reduced the gap between the completed canal here and at Marsden so that a connection of a kind was possible using packhorses to carry goods transhipped to and from the boats. Trade continued in that way until the canal was eventually complete but toll receipts were low. As a major trans-Pennine artery the canal plus packhorses could hardly be considered a success.

The Huddersfield Canal Co. was really running out of steam or, more to the point, money and work was coming almost to a halt. The national situation was discouraging. Napoleon had taken control in France and Income Tax was introduced to pay for the war. The years 1799 to 1801 saw bad harvests and famine. Casks of salted herrings were sent from Hull to feed the poor in the upper Tame Valley where conditions were so desperate that the Saddleworth Vestry feared there would be rioting. Contingents of the Royal Huddersfield Fusiliers and the Halifax Voluntary Troop of Cavalry were sent to keep the peace.

Outram was aware that the Huddersfield Canal Co. was not alone in its difficulties. He advised the Worcester & Birmingham Canal Co. on a temporary tramway while the company raised the money to complete the Tardebigge Tunnel and the many locks on the route to Worcester – not that they could afford the tramway; and he had given advice to the Stratford Canal Co., who were so hard-pressed that it took them twenty-three years to build their canal. Nearer home the Leeds & Liverpool, although started in 1770, was still incomplete and would not be finished until five years after the Huddersfield. The company did not renew Nicholas Brown's contract in February 1799. He had not been a success as resident engineer, failing to ensure that work was properly carried out and allowing errors in the construction of locks and incorrect levels at by-wash weirs. To what extent that was because of inexperience, or a lack of competence, or because the company had never been willing to provide the qualified assistants he desperately needed, I cannot say. At least the experience was useful to him as he later successfully practised as a land surveyor in partnership with his son in Wakefield. William Bailiffe had his salary increased to £200 per year and took on responsibility for all of the canal.

Disastrous floods following heavy rainstorms knocked the canal back completely in the summer of 1799. Water overtopped the embankment of the reservoir at Tunnel End, Marsden, causing the embankment to give way and the township of Marsden to be flooded. The reservoir at Slaithwaite was only saved from collapse by cutting away part of the embankment to let the water drain away. Aqueducts over the River Colne at Tunnel End and over the River Tame at Stalybridge were swept away in the flood. There was damage all along the canal.

All of the original share capital authorised by Parliament had been used up and the company could not afford to pay its workers. As work slowed to a halt in 1800 only those owed less than £30 in arrears of wages were paid, with amounts in excess of that to be paid at a rate of only 5s (25p) in the pound. Like many other canal companies they had to go back to Parliament for authority to raise more money. A second Act of Parliament in 1800 allowed the raising of a further £20 per share issued. The investors may not originally have envisaged these dire circumstances or that the company would have a right to call on them for more money. That right was of little purpose, however, if the shareholders' pockets were empty because of the problems brought on by the war. Work on the tunnel all but stopped. The company had itself carried out work at the eastern end using labour directly employed by them. Thomas Lee, under contract to build the first 1,000 yards (914m) from the Diggle end, had fallen behind the work rate expected and in 1797, when offered an increased rate per yard dug, he would not accept the new terms. He was dismissed after driving only half of the contracted length. George Evans, who had worked on the centre part of the tunnel since 1796, walked away from the job in 1798 rather than lose money. In 1799 Outram himself offered to take on responsibility for construction of the tunnel. The company had not decided on his offer when the floods put paid to the idea; they had far too many other problems and Outram withdrew his offer.

The Rochdale Canal was in similar difficulties, with the central section between Littleborough and Todmorden incomplete and money hard to come by. By 1801 prices of

Packhorses were normally led in teams of about thirty horses. It would have taken at least 150 horses to carry the load of a short Huddersfield Canal narrow boat over Standedge, depending on the weight of the load and its ability to be divided in packs between the horses. *(Keith Gibson)*

general household commodities were near double their cost in 1793 when Outram prepared his estimate of costs. If building materials prices increased in line with that, no matter how good Outram's estimate had been, or how well the construction had been managed, every ton of sand, every ton of lime, every ounce of gunpowder for blasting the rock away would cost almost twice as much as he had originally allowed.

The Peak Forest Canal had been complete since August 1800, apart from the locks at Marple where a temporary tramway worked until the locks opened in October 1805. With trade all along the line of their canals the proprietors of the Peak Forest and Ashton Canals were anxious to extend trade into Yorkshire. In December 1800 Outram was asked to consider a tramway over Standedge to link the incomplete canal – but nothing came of the idea. When a delegation from the Ashton Company, led by Manchester merchant John Rooth, met the Huddersfield Canal Co., Rooth offered to carry goods on the incomplete canal between Huddersfield and Manchester himself if warehouses were provided and the Huddersfield Company would lend him £500 to start up the business. The Ashton Canal Co. went so far as to lend him £1,500 to build a warehouse in Manchester. His brother William, the Manager of the Aire & Calder Navigation, was a member of the Committee of the Huddersfield Canal Co. John Rooth obviously impressed the Huddersfield people, as in 1801 they asked him to act as Superintendent of the Ashton-Dobcross length of the canal and, soon afterwards, of all of the canal at a salary of £300 per year. Although the Huddersfield Canal Co. never had his full attention, as he also ran his own canal carrying business, John Rooth & Co., the company was obviously satisfied. They even agreed to provide six boats on hire – four west of the Pennines, and two to the east – so that he could enlarge his fleet. Perhaps that was not entirely altruistic, as they would benefit from increased tolls if he generated trade on the canal.

In 1801 Benjamin Outram resigned from his canal interests to concentrate on managing the Butterley Ironworks. He would only live for a further four years, dying suddenly at the age of forty-one and tragically leaving his widow to pay off borrowings from the Butterley Ironworks that had paid for an extravagant lifestyle. He has been much criticised for his failure to accurately cost the work. Hindsight is a wonderful thing! There was no way that he could have foreseen that, after a long period of relative stability, prices would almost double in the period of eight years after he estimated the costs. His estimate was based on generalised rates for the tasks involved rather than on a detailed survey and design. Not ideal – but it was the way these things were done. Even today promoters of major developments delay paying high professional fees for detailed design as long as possible; the promoters of canal schemes were certainly not going to pay those costs until they had permission to proceed from Parliament. Outram did not supervise Nicholas Brown or ensure work was carried out in a planned way. That was not his job. He was only contracted to provide a limited service to the company and only a few days on site after he had delivered plans and specifications. He had provided the plans of the proposed works and he had reported to the Committee of the huddersfiled Canal Co. in accordance with his contract. He even attempted to resolve the issue of Standedge Tunnel once and for all by offering to complete it himself.

With Outram resigned and Brown dismissed, William Bailiffe left the company's employment in February 1801. They had no engineer but there was precious little money to do engineering work with. Rooth shepherded what he could of the toll receipts, brought in what money he could of that owed by shareholders and began to bring some order to the company's affairs. He had to take on the unofficial role of engineer – unqualified and unpaid. Work on the tunnel took second place to keeping the canal working after the floods of 1799. Locks, reservoirs and bridges had to be repaired or rebuilt because of flood damage or because some were badly built in the first place. The water supply reservoirs were unsatisfactory. Not only had the spillway arrangements at Tunnel End and Slaithwaite reservoirs been inadequate in 1799, but a partially completed reservoir on the moor at Swinshore Common had been so damaged that it was abandoned.

In 1802 peace in the war with France was achieved through the Treaty of Amiens. The weavers and clothiers expressed their relief by erecting a stone column in the neighbouring Holme Valley to the south of the Colne Valley where it still stands in the centre of the town of Holmfirth. Their relief, and whatever relief the Canal Company felt, was misplaced. War resumed in 1803, and the problems for the woollen weavers and clothiers returned with a vengeance. Trade was seriously depressed for many years, not recovering until 1812. Even the Committee members of the company were not immune. John Plowes was bankrupt. The company had been considering a tender to complete the tunnel from John Varley, who was employed on flood repairs, but decided not to proceed. Such limited work as took place on the tunnel was by the company's own efforts.

Until the tunnel was complete the canal would remain a poor affair providing a local service to the two valleys only, and two valleys whose staple trade had been knocked for six by the French wars. The problem had to be resolved somehow and the company appointed John Booth of Oldham as tunnel inspector to assist Rooth. In November 1802 David Whitehead, a surveyor who worked with Outram on the Peak Forest Canal, was asked to check the accuracy of the alignment and level of what had been built. A wise move – as he found the working face at the Marsden end was being cut downwards. Worse, the invert at the Diggle entrance was higher than that at the Marsden entrance. These errors had to be put right, requiring excavation of the tunnel to a greater depth at Diggle where the stone arch lining had to be taken down and rebuilt. The company hoped to restart work in the central section of the tunnel but only one contractor, Jonathan Woodhouse of Ashby de la Zouch, could be found who was willing to take on the work. His ideas of the likely cost were considerably more than the company was able to pay.

The rival Rochdale Canal was opened in 1804, but the external climate was improving as the tide of war turned in Britain's favour. Nelson defeated a Franco/Spanish fleet at Trafalgar, losing his own life in the battle, and the extension of war beyond Europe would see Britain take over French colonies in India and the Far East. The war was still ruinously expensive with the export trade lost difficult to recover but, with victories at last and prices no longer increasing, light began to be seen at the end of the tunnel, and with stronger leadership provided by John Rooth, the Canal Company determined that light should be seen through its own tunnel.

In 1806 a third Act of Parliament was granted allowing the company to raise a further £100,000 to pay off its debts and finish the canal. Work had continued slowly at the ends of the tunnel since John Booth's appointment but the driving of about one third of the tunnel had still not begun. If a contractor could not be found the company needed engineering expertise. They went to the best man available. Thomas Telford was the rising man and he was asked to report on the work required to complete the canal. He was the Surveyor of Public Works to the county of Shropshire where he had been involved with William Jessop on the Ellesmere Canal (now known as the Llangollen Canal) with its magnificent aqueduct at Pontcysyllte completed in 1805. And he had surveyed improvements to roads and bridges in the Scottish Highlands, where he was also the principle engineer for the Caledonian Canal through the Great Glen between Fort William and Inverness. He would become the eminent engineer of the last phase of the canal era.

Telford presented his report to a Special General Assembly of the Proprietors on 21 January 1807. Dealing first with the tunnel, he listed the work required and set out an order of work to be done with dates for completion of each main task. Less than 20% of the tunnel was complete, about 60% was broken through but incomplete and slightly more than 20% was completely undriven through the rock strata. If the company worked to his schedule the tunnel would be complete in December 1810 at a cost of a further £45,000. He priced the canal between Wool Road, Dobcross and the tunnel at Diggle and suggested that three locks be built here in 1807, four in 1808 and the last in 1809. He also recommended repairs and alterations to the existing works and looked at the water supply to the canal. He was critical of the reservoirs, regretting 'that such large sums of money have been expended on such narrow dingles' and recommended that an additional reservoir be built. To complete the canal would cost £82,498.

Telford's report had the advantages of clarity and certainty. It spelled out exactly what had to be done with a timetable and sequence of tasks. Unlike Outram, who had written for Parliamentary approval or provided plans for Brown to detail on site, or Whitworth, who had written specifically for a lay committee, Telford was writing both to a lay committee and to provide John Rooth and John Booth with a set of instructions. He could report in more detail and with more certainty about the tunnel than the earlier reports. More work had been carried out revealing the issues, and the workings were no longer subject to the ingress of large amounts of water. The Canal Company may have been dismayed at what all this would cost but it was hardly a shock and they acted with a surprising firmness of purpose. Rooth was authorised to act on Telford's recommendation. Unlike Nicholas Brown, he had the support of the Committee. He also had, in John Booth, someone to share the load with and, now most of the canal was built and a limited income coming in from tolls, they were able to concentrate on the major tasks remaining. The catastrophic price rises of earlier years had ended. Prices remained high but they were stable and Telford's costs remained accurate.

Telford's instructions were followed to the letter with work completed to the timescale he recommended. In June 1809 Rooth was at last able to report to the General Assembly of Proprietors that 'the tunnel (was) perforated, and the line and level agree.' But nothing was easy in building this canal. The embankment at the eastern end of Black Moss reservoir breached. Water rushed into the Colne Valley in the early morning of 29 November 1810. This 'Black Flood' destroyed homes and mill buildings in Marsden, where six people lost their lives, and flooded low-lying land almost to Huddersfield. The *Gentlemen's Magazine* for December 1810 reported the tragic story of James Bamforth and his wife. Washed from their bed by the flood, he managed to wedge his body between the jambs of the window but he was not strong enough to hold his wife. Her body was found several miles downstream.

Shortly after this on 10 December the company sent a boat though the tunnel for the first time. At last the company had a complete canal with water from end to end. Instead of being on branch canals, off the Calder & Hebble in the east or the Ashton Canal in the west, the Colne and Tame valleys were on a cross-country route.

On 4 April 1811 – seventeen years to the day since the original Act of Parliament – the company organised a celebration the like of which had never been seen before in Diggle and Marsden. A crowd estimated at about 10,000 people met at Diggle. They saw a party of 500 invited guests – presumably the 'Great and the Good' of Lancashire and Yorkshire, as that is the usual way with these things – embark on a fleet of boats. They were taken through the tunnel to the strains of a band playing *Rule Britannia* that accompanied them to Marsden. Here, an equally enthusiastic crowd met the guests as they emerged from the tunnel. The party was taken to Huddersfield for dinner at The George Inn.

The company had eventually built a twenty-mile-long (32km) canal through what were then two rural Pennine upland valleys, with forty-two locks on the east between Huddersfield and Marsden and thirty-two locks on the west between Ashton-under-Lyne and Diggle, each with a rise of about 10ft. Unlike most canals whose locks are numbered in sequence from one end to the other, the Huddersfield locks are numbered between Ashton and Diggle as lock Nos 1W-32W and from Huddersfield to Marsden as 1E-42E. There were other engineering features of interest – bridges, aqueducts and two short tunnels at Whitelands and Scout – but nothing to compare to the immense tunnel at Standedge, 3 miles 135 yards (4.9km) long.

By far the longest canal tunnel ever built in Britain, it was also on the highest summit level reached by a British canal at 645ft (196m) above sea level. Ironically an even longer tunnel nearly three and a half miles (5.6km) long was officially opened by Napoleon Bonaparte at Riqueval on the Canal de Saint Quentin in north-east France in 1810 – the very same year that Standedge was completed. So Standedge was only the second longest canal tunnel then built – never the longest. Riqueval, however, is cut through a much easier landscape and not being far below the surface was not an engineering challenge of the same magnitude. Unlike Standedge, Riqueval never closed but, like Standedge today, boats are taken through in convoys by electric tugs. An even longer French tunnel now closed after a roof collapse, the Souterrain de Rove between the Etang de Berre and Marseilles, at four and a half miles (7.3km), relegated Standedge to third place in the canal tunnel league. To say that Standedge was the Channel Tunnel of its day underestimates the difficulty of the task. The Channel Tunnel is ten times the length and consists of three parallel tunnels that were driven in three and a half years. Although an immense and expensive task, it was not so difficult for the teams of experts involved as was Standedge in terms of the knowledge and experience available to Outram. Unlike the Channel Tunnel, Standedge is not straight. The difficulties of surveying a line over the moor and transferring that to the working faces hundreds of feet below were too much for the engineering and surveying abilities available in the construction of the tunnel. At the centre it is as much as 26ft (7.9m) to the north-west of the true centre line. It was mainly rock-faced with jagged edges leaving the shot and tool marks of the workers in view. Unstable rock was supported in places by a stone-arched lining. Although built to the minimum dimensions possible to keep down the cost, there were three 'Wides' or passing places along its length.

Outram replaced the stone-built aqueduct over the River Tame at Stalybridge, destroyed in the flood of 1799, by a pre-fabricated iron trough after building a similar structure on the Derby Canal. The ironwork was cast at the Butterley Ironworks and assembled on site. There was then insufficient knowledge of the behaviour of such structures and the design proved inadequate but it stood until 1875. It had then sagged to such an extent that cross-braced rods were added to the outside of the trough and a tie rod connecting it to the towpath, which was unique in being carried on a separate traditional stone-bridge over the river, rather than as part of the iron aqueduct. The aqueduct remains today as the oldest metal aqueduct in use.

The water supply to the canal was provided from a series of reservoirs. Brun Clough, Black Moss, Little Black Moss, Diggle and Red Brook were built in the hills between Diggle and Marsden, but the embankment to that at Tunnel End was adjacent to the Marsden Tunnel mouth and Sparth and Slaithwaite reservoirs were further down the Colne Valley. Black Moss, whose bank collapse caused the 'Black Flood' in Marsden, was not repaired until 1816.

Standedge Tunnel – an unlined bare rock section. *(HCS)*

Standedge Tunnel – a stone-lined section. *(HCS)*

Stalybridge Aqueduct, with the iron trough in the foreground and the stone towpath bridge beyond. Note the change in height of the parapet wall following rebuilding at the former County boundary between Lancashire and Cheshire. *(HCS)*

Swellands, recommended by Telford to replace that at Swinshore Common abandoned in 1799, was proposed, but the site was not bought until 1819 and it was not completed until 1825.

The canal had been built partly by contractors and partly by direct labour employed by the company. As many as fifty men lost their lives in its construction – mainly in the tunnel, like the sadly aptly named George Spark who, together with his colleague Thomas Whitehead, was killed by an explosion in 1803. The methods of working in the tunnel would horrify Health and Safety Inspectors today. A hole was drilled by hand with an auger; it was dried thoroughly, then packed with gunpowder and sealed with clay. The fuse was lit and the workers retreated to what they hoped was a safe distance. Assuming all went well, they were then able to break the shattered material away with picks and shovels for it to be lifted up a construction shaft to the hillside above. The whole process depended on unknown factors determining the force of the explosion – the amount of powder inserted into the hole, the amount of clay sealing it and how well that seal held the charge in place, the nature of the rock and its likelihood to shatter or split into large sections. A similar process was used for boring the construction shafts except that, after setting the charge and lighting the fuse, the workers clung precariously to a rope that was quickly hauled up the shaft on their signal. And all of this was carried out by candlelight.

The spoil lifted from the tunnel up the construction shafts can still be seen today from the main road over Standedge, although most of what is there came from the later railway tunnels. The method of construction from these shafts was an amazing feat involving the building of miles of temporary water supply adits to power 'water engines' used for lifting spoil to the surface. Taken from the mining industry, these machines were powered by the weight of a heavy water-filled barrel released down a balance pit alongside the main shaft. The weight of the barrel was sufficient to lift spoil up the much deeper main shaft via a system of pulley gearing. At the bottom of the balance pit an adit was dug to allow the barrel to be emptied, so reversing the process. The scale of these works was enormously costly. Underground adits for draining the balance pits added up to a quarter of the length of the tunnel itself. Not surprisingly the company tried other methods – waterwheels and steam engines but they were not a success, although steam-powered pumps were used to drain the workings hundreds of feet below. A total of thirty-one construction shafts were started – fourteen to build the canal (including two at Red Brook where, following mining practice, water was sprayed down a secondary shaft offset from the line of the canal to encourage ventilation of the workings) and seventeen in the construction of the drainage adits – but not all were completed as lack of money and drainage problems caused changes of plans.

The origin of the men working on the canal is unknown apart from evidence in the Parish registers, but the muscle power of these 'navvies' – so-called because their predecessors had built the river navigations – built the canal. They lived in primitive shacks near the workings. Some built on Standedge were more permanent. Stone-built cottages were provided for overlookers and skilled craftsmen such as carpenters and blacksmiths. The workmen were not so lucky, living in a wooden hut shanty town nearby together with their wives and families. They even managed to drain and cultivate an area of land to grow potatoes – although I doubt that was very productive on the acid peat soil at this altitude.

In June 1812 it was reported to the General Assembly of Proprietors that the canal had cost £402,653 including £123,804 for Standedge Tunnel. Outram's estimate had been £182,748, of which £55,187 would be required to build the tunnel. Other canals showed the same phenomenon of costs rising as construction proceeded – indeed it was the norm. Possibly engineers were over-optimistic, more likely there were unforeseen factors: problems of draining water from the workings and as happened at Standedge; problems caused by apparently vindictive nature – like the floods that affected the building of this canal – and problems of poor management that certainly affected this canal. All the canals built at this time were widely out in their eventual cost compared to the original estimate because of the huge inflation of prices. If Outram's original estimate had allowed for that inflation he would inevitably have calculated the total cost at more than £300,000. If the company had paid more in the first place to give Nicholas Brown qualified assistants and managed the excavation of the tunnel better, the final cost might have been nearer to that. But they had completed their canal, unlike the Salisbury & Southampton Canal, thirteen miles of which were built before work was abandoned without reaching either destination. Or the Dorset & Somerset Canal that only managed to build eight out of the eleven miles of a branch between Nettlebridge and Frome and never started work on the main line before the money ran out.

3 The Working Years

The canal was open for business. Just as it had been a bad time to build a canal, so it was an equally bad time to operate a canal, particularly here where the staple trade had been so hard hit. Napoleon had been defeated in Russia in 1812, but the war continued, the cost remained high and export trade remained disrupted.

It was not easy to break into the pattern of through trade established since the Rochdale Canal opened seven years earlier, especially as the new canal was hard for the boaters. Both canals were heavily locked. The Rochdale was far from direct, taking a broad sweep to the north, but it avoided the need for a long summit tunnel worked by the boatmen 'legging' the boat through (laying on the deck, and walking on the tunnel walls). Tolls were less to use the Rochdale. Only one company was involved. To go from the Calder & Hebble to Manchester via the Huddersfield involved paying tolls to Sir John Ramsden's Canal, the Huddersfield and the Ashton Canals – and even to the Rochdale if the journey extended to the Bridgewater Canal.

And the Rochdale was a broad canal. Transhipment of goods was not entirely avoided because 70ft (21m) boats from the west had to transfer loads to shorter 57ft (17.3m) Calder & Hebble-size vessels at Sowerby Bridge, but these West Country Keels (as they became known when the Aire & Calder was enlarged for longer boats) could traverse the entire waterway and trade into Manchester or beyond on the Bridgewater Canal. The Huddersfield and the connecting Ashton were narrow canals. A classic break of gauge situation existed in Huddersfield. A narrow boat could trade on the Huddersfield Canal to Aspley Basin but was too long for the short locks of Sir John Ramsden's Canal. A West Country Keel could also reach Aspley but it was too wide for the narrow locks and bridges beyond. That was of no consequence for trade to the narrow Midlands canals, but most long-distance trade was to Manchester or the ports of Liverpool and Hull. As early as June 1811 the company instructed John Rooth to have two narrow boats shortened so that they could trade onto the Calder & Hebble and the following year the first of a small fleet of short narrow boats was built.

Trade may have been more limited than the company hoped, and much of local origin, but one-way working was required at Standedge. The tunnel's long single-track bore was hardly the best place to meet a boat moving in the opposite direction; the three 'wides', or passing places (White Horse, Old Judy and Red Brook) – with a fourth (Brun Clough) added later – were a long way apart especially when the only means of propulsion was 'legging'. A by-law was introduced in 1812 allowing entry at Marsden in the early morning and late afternoon only.

The war ended with France's defeat by Wellington at Waterloo in 1815. By 1819 toll income at £7,924 was increasing. Goods carried then, and through the working life of the canal, included coal, corn and stone – especially limestone, used to treat acid upland soils and, when converted to lime, essential to builders for mortar and plaster before cement mortars came into regular use. General merchandise was the major item carried – not coal which topped the list on most waterways – much of it, no doubt, being bales of wool and cotton or bundles of cloth that were so important to trade here. John Rooth's own company, J. Rooth & Co., was the principal carrier on the canal.

Maintenance was vital to keep the canal open and Nicholas Brown came back in favour, being appointed as engineer in 1814. He was allowed to spend money, not just on maintaining

Broad-beam Calder & Hebble boats at the Wharf, Aspley, Huddersfield, on the arm of the Huddersfield Broad Canal leading to the Huddersfield Narrow. The stone-built warehouse is converted to flats, but the timber-built warehouse (on the left) has been demolished, and the site now forms part of the University campus. Wakefield Road Bridge and Aspley Basin are beyond. *(Trevor Ellis collection)*

the locks and banks of the canal, but also on the water supply. He was replaced by John Raistrick in 1818. Raistrick told the General Assembly that year that locks were still in 'a wretched condition' and there were many leaks to fix. The poor financial state of the company was now publicly blamed on John Rooth. He had left the company's employment in June of the previous year when the company decided they needed a younger man. He had been a pillar of society in the Saddleworth area, even building the Navigation Inn at Wool Road. At sixty years of age he moved to look after his family colliery and ironworks interests in the Black Country.

Water supply was a problem. Complaints that the flow in the River Tame was insufficient to drive the water-powered mills led Nicholas Brown to improve reservoirs and feeder channels in 1814. Black Moss reservoir had not been repaired or Swellands started, and the canal was closed by a lack of water for thirty-nine days in 1818. Raistrick was concerned about the stability of the short Whitelands Tunnel in Ashton but the company did not sanction its repair until 1824. Being only just below the surface it was then opened out rather than repaired; the canal remains in a narrow channel here to this day.

John Bower, who succeeded Rooth as agent, saw that the company needed warehouses to attract trade from goods awaiting transhipment. The rental income would boost the company's earnings. Warehouses in Manchester and Wakefield might persuade canal carriers to use the Huddersfield route. In 1820 a warehouse was bought in Manchester and in 1823 a warehouse was built in Wakefield. A second Manchester warehouse was built soon afterwards at Ducie Street alongside the Ashton Canal and a second warehouse in Wakefield followed. Further warehouses were built at Stalybridge, Wool Road (Dobcross), Marsden and at Engine Bridge (the present Chapel Hill bridge), Huddersfield.

Standedge Tunnel remained a bottleneck. Boats took three or four hours to be 'legged' through while the horse was led over the top of the hill. One may think that few horses would be taken over the hill and that, having 'legged' through the tunnel, the boatmen would pick up a new animal that spent its life confined to towing on the west or east side only. This canal

The long since demolished warehouse at Wool Road, Dobcross. *(HCS)*

was mainly the province of small carriers who could not afford the luxury of spare animals, however. The provision of a steam-powered tug was considered in 1816 and again in 1822 when the company paid a Mr Wharton £50 to experiment with a tug. But that came to nothing and John Raistrick was authorised to provide a tug owned by the company. This hauled convoys of boats through the tunnel along a chain in the canal bed for a time in the late 1820s but 'legging' soon resumed.

As the economy improved, tolls began to rise. The company finally caught up with maintenance of the canal. The Committee reported to the General Assembly of Proprietors in June 1823 that they hoped to declare a dividend in the following year. Shareholders remaining from the formation of the company thirty years before would certainly agree with the description of the company in their report as 'this hitherto unfortunate undertaking'. A dividend of £1 per share was paid in 1824, to be followed by a similar amount in 1825. This would not to be repeated until 1830. The company had heavy expenditure in 1825, finally bringing Swellands reservoir into use and working on an extension to Red Brook reservoir. Then the textile trade was hit in 1825 and 1826 by a slump so severe that the bank of Messrs Harrop & Co. in Dobcross suspended payments for a time. In fact 1826 was a bad year for the canal altogether. Traffic was stopped for twenty-one days with the canal frozen up in January and, apart from the Ashton to Wool Road section, the canal was closed by a lack of water for sixty-two days in July and August.

Trade recovered. The 1830s saw the company become increasingly prosperous and pay off debts. Toll income reached £20,543 by the end of the decade. Dividends were paid: 10s (50p) in 1830, £1 in 1831 and 1832, £1 10s (£1.50p) in 1833, 1834 and 1835, £1 15s (£1.75p) in 1836, and £2 each year from 1837 to 1842.

A new warehouse was built in Ashton-under-Lyne in 1833 and a second warehouse at Engine Bridge, Huddersfield. Near to this they also built a house for John Raistrick who was now acting as Agent and Superintendent as well as engineer. At last able to tackle the long-standing problem of water supply, he recommended an additional reservoir be built above Tunnel End at March Haigh which was completed in 1838.

Public wharves were open at Ashton-under-Lyne, Stalybridge, Mossley, Wool Road (Dobcross), Diggle, Marsden, Slaithwaite, Milnsbridge and Huddersfield. In 1830 the Huddersfield Shipping Co. advertised 'flyboats daily to Saddleworth, Ashton-under-Lyne,

Oldham, Stockport and Manchester, whence goods are forwarded to Liverpool, Chester and to all parts of the South of England.' White's Directory listed the canal carriers trading daily from Huddersfield in 1837 as Buckley, Kershaw & Co. (to Hull, Manchester and Liverpool), Carver, Driver & Co. (to Manchester, Liverpool, Dewsbury etc.), John Kenworthy & Co. (to London, Manchester, Stafford etc.), T&W Marsden (to Manchester, Liverpool, Hull etc.), Deacon & Co. (to London etc.) and Pickford & Co. (to London, Birmingham, Bristol, Manchester etc.). Buckley, Kershaw was the successor to J. Rooth & Co. – Rooth having passed control to his manager, Edmund Buckley, in 1811, and Buckley bringing in his Manchester agent, William Kershaw, in 1826. The company remained the principal carrier on the canal. In 1826 William Rooth, who retained an interest, noted that the company had three full-size narrow boats and

Frenches Wharf, Greenfield. *(HCS)*

Wade Lock, Uppermill. *(Trevor Ellis collection)*

ten short boats able to trade onto the Calder & Hebble. In 1838 Pigot & Sons' Directory listed Wool Road, as having: 'Conveyance by water to London, and all intermediate places daily.' The canal here was used by thirty boats a day. There was even smuggling on the canal. Residents of Slaithwaite were known as 'Moonrakers' after customs officials found men fishing in the canal. They claimed to be catching the reflection of the moon and denied any knowledge of contraband that had been quietly dropped in the water.

Congestion at Standedge Tunnel still occupied the company. Rather than allow boaters to 'leg' through themselves at varying speeds, the canal company employed their own 'leggers' from 1833. The downside to this was a charge of 1s 6d (7.5p) for each trip through the tunnel.

The long-suffering shareholders may have been delighted at receiving a regular return on their investment at last but the glory days would not last. A more formidable competitor than the Rochdale Canal was on the horizon – the steam railway. When George Stephenson built the Stockton & Darlington Railway in 1825, and followed that in 1829 with the Liverpool to Manchester railway, the writing was on the wall for canal companies. Speculation in railway company shares became another way to a quick profit as more and more lines were projected. Indeed the railway mania of the 1840s far outstretched the canal mania of fifty years before.

In 1841 the Manchester & Leeds Railway opened following a course parallel to the Rochdale Canal and the Calder & Hebble Navigation between Manchester and Wakefield, then continuing to Normanton where it made a connection to Leeds. The Rochdale Canal Co. responded in the only way open to it – by cutting toll rates. The Huddersfield Canal Co. had no choice but to follow suit. No dividend would be declared that year or, indeed, ever again.

At first the railways succeeded with an almost entirely new trade, passengers, and canals retained their trade in goods, especially bulk goods such as coal, but only by cutting toll rates. Profits rapidly disappeared and canal shareholders were only too willing to sell out to railway companies, often before the railway was built. The railway companies favoured buying up canals where they could too; there were obvious advantages in controlling the competition. Many canals came under railway control but they proved something of a mixed blessing for their new owners. The canals had been established with public rights of navigation by Acts of Parliament and the authority of Parliament was required for a railway company to purchase a canal company. Clauses were included in the resulting Acts to ensure that the railway honoured public rights of navigation and kept the canals in good order.

The Ashton and Peak Forest Canals passed into the ownership of the Sheffield, Ashton-under-Lyne & Manchester Railway. That company brought the iron road nearer to the Huddersfield Canal when its main line from Manchester reached Guide Bridge to the south of Ashton-under-Lyne in November 1841, only eight months after the completion of the Manchester & Leeds. Two alternative routes to Stalybridge were soon underway. The Sheffield, Ashton-under-Lyne & Manchester Railway was extending from Guide Bridge, and the Ashton, Sheffield & Liverpool Railway was building a link between Stalybridge, Ashton-under-Lyne and the Manchester & Leeds Railway at Miles Platting. Both would open by the end of 1846.

Before that, on the other side of the Pennines, the Manchester & Leeds Railway had proposed a branch from its main line to Huddersfield but, providing no access to the west, this was not popular in the town and the company did not proceed. At the same time the Leeds, Dewsbury & Manchester Co. proposed a direct link between Leeds and Huddersfield through Dewsbury to by-pass the circuitous Manchester and Leeds route. The Huddersfield & Manchester Co. proposed to continue this route up the Colne Valley through a tunnel at Standedge and via the Tame Valley to link with the railways proposed to Stalybridge. These railways would provide a direct link between Manchester and Leeds and connect the growing town of Huddersfield to the railway network.

The shareholders and Committee members of the Huddersfield Canal Co. cannot have relished the prospect of competition from a railway parallel to the canal and the railway clearly did not want competition from the canal. In May 1844 a Special General Assembly of Proprietors was called at which the terms on which the railway company offered to purchase the canal company were reported. Railway shares originally issued at a value of £30 were offered in exchange for Huddersfield Canal Co. shares to acquire the company at a total cost of £180,885. With canal shares valued at no more than £8-£9 the shareholders must have counted their blessings. This generous offer guaranteed success in acquiring the company.

The Leeds, Dewsbury & Manchester Railway was authorised by Parliament on 30 June 1845 and the Huddersfield & Manchester on 21 July 1845 with the latter Act also authorising the merger with the canal company. A new company, the Huddersfield and Manchester Railway & Canal Co., was formed and the Huddersfield Canal Co. wound up. A final General Assembly of Proprietors was told that the company had eventually paid off its debts and the business was transferred to the new company free of any such charge.

Railways promoted as local concerns rapidly amalgamated to form larger companies, and the two new railways both sold out to the London & North-Western Railway (LNWR). That left things a little complicated around Huddersfield. The LNWR needed to cross over the Manchester and Leeds tracks near the junction of Sir John Ramsden's Canal and the Calder & Hebble Navigation. The Manchester and Leeds needed access along the proposed LNWR line to reach a branch it was building from Huddersfield to Penistone that would join the Sheffield, Ashton-under-Lyne & Manchester Railway to gain access south to Sheffield. Also the Lancashire & Yorkshire, as the Manchester & Leeds would soon become, was anxious that some of its trains from the Calder Valley could reach Leeds via the shorter LNWR route. The two companies agreed on running rights over each others tracks and to jointly build the new station in Huddersfield.

The LNWR extended its canal ownership by purchasing Sir John Ramsden's Canal, known thereafter as the Huddersfield Broad Canal, from the Ramsden Estate for £45,134 13s 4d. It was soon apparent that the railway company had paid over the odds for the Huddersfield Narrow Canal, as the Huddersfield Canal became known, for a very good reason. Control of the canal made construction of the tunnel at Standedge far easier and quicker. By building the railway tunnel close to and parallel to the canal Joseph Locke, the engineer to the LNWR, and Alfred Jee, his assistant who actually did the work on the railway between Huddersfield and Stalybridge (and also started a sideline running his own canal carrying business at Marsden, hiring to the tunnel contractors), knew what strata they had to excavate and, by driving connecting adits, it was possible to use the canal tunnel to take out spoil from the two ends and by hauling it up the remaining construction shafts.

The railway was open from Leeds to Huddersfield on 2 August 1845. Canal enthusiasts standing in front of the magnificent classical frontage of Huddersfield Station making a pilgrimage to The George Inn to see the birthplace of the Huddersfield Canal should not be misled by The George Hotel in St George's Square in front of the station. The Square and the streets between here and the Market Place were laid out as a successful piece of town planning speculation by the Ramsden Estate when the railway opened. The George Inn was demolished to make way for John William Street. Its façade was re-erected on St Peter's Street where it remains today.

The railway was opened to Manchester on 1 August 1849. It had a double-track layout throughout except for the single-track tunnel at Standedge. Because the railway company had been able to use the canal tunnel and its construction shafts, the hillside had been perforated from end to end in only twenty-three months, but the spirit of Benjamin Outram must have managed an angelic smile when the tunnel cost £201,608 compared to Jee's estimate of £147,240.

Just as the canal company had celebrated, so did the railway – with a huge picnic at Diggle on 13 July 1849. Journey times were dramatically reduced; the first timetables showed a time of only 1 hour 25 minutes from Manchester to Huddersfield, or 1 hour 15 minutes by express, and Standedge Tunnel was traversed in only 9 minutes. The railway company even took advantage of the canal by arranging a water supply for its engines at Huddersfield Station from the canal reservoir at Slaithwaite.

*Above: T*he magnificent classical frontage of Huddersfield Railway Station, designed by the York architect J.P. Pritchett for the London North Western & Lancashire and Yorkshire Railway Companies. *(Kathryn Gibson)*

Right: The façade of the George Inn, Huddersfield - the location of the inaugural meeting of the Huddersfield Canal Company. It was rebuilt in St Peter's Street when the Inn was demolished to make way for John William Street between the Market Place and the railway station at St George's Square. *(Kathryn Gibson)*

The railway company had every reason to maintain traffic on the canal so as to maximise the profit of its purchase until the railway came into use. 169,487 tons were carried in 1848 before the opening of the railway. Forty years later the equivalent figure was 179,786 tons. There had been no actual loss of trade, but the total tonnage carried by rail and canal had increased several times over in this period of rapid industrial growth. The new trade was carried by rail but the canal remained viable for bulk goods, particularly coal to feed the boilers of the much larger textile mills being built, as the industry took advantage of the growing population and expanding markets.

Not only were canal tolls reduced to meet competition from the railways, the carriers too had to cut their rates or go out of business. National carrier Pickford's transferred their loads to rail in 1846. Other carriers cut the wages of the boatmen and owner boatmen accepted smaller remunerations. Boatmen started to take their families to live on board to avoid the costs of a separate land-based home and having to pay crew. What we think of as the traditional canal narrow boat, with a small living cabin only 10ft (3.04m) long at the back of the boat, developed at this time. Before that the boats were simple open vessels with no cabin or only a small shelter for the boatmen to sleep in when away from home.

To add to the boatmens' problems, the canal suffered from extreme weather conditions. It was closed because of flooding in 1834, 1856, 1861, 1866 and 1872 and summer droughts played havoc with water supplies. The canal was closed for eight days in 1849, for thirty-five days in 1852, for twenty-three days in 1853, for sixty-six days in 1866, for seventy days in 1869, for forty-one days in 1870, and from June right through to November in 1884. Standedge Tunnel was closed for repairs for eighty-six days in 1857 causing the Aire & Calder Navigation to complain at the obstruction to trade.

In the early years of railway control the LNWR did not discourage trade. Like the canal the railway suffered from a bottleneck: the single-track tunnel at Standedge. A second tunnel was built between April 1868 and October 1871 in much the same way as before using the canal tunnel and its construction shafts to remove spoil. Halfway through, the two railway tunnels were linked in a large cavern known as the Cathedral. Construction was not without its problems; in November 1868 a boat sank after hitting fallen rock caused by blasting in the railway tunnel. Steam tugs used by the railway company were suspected of damaging the tunnel. A boatload of gunpowder exploded the following year killing two boatmen.

Traffic continued to increase on the railway. Delays caused by heavy coal trains to faster passenger trains led to capacity being doubled by widening to four tracks in the Colne Valley and the building of a duplicate route, the Micklehurst Loop, on the south-east side of the Tame Valley. Then a new double-track railway tunnel was built – the fourth tunnel through Standedge – and on a much larger scale. Most of the mounds of spoil still to be seen, albeit grassed over, in Marsden and Diggle and, still bleak mounds, on Standedge are from this tunnel. The spoil was mainly taken by convoys of boats towed by steam tugs to be dumped at the ends of the tunnel, but some was hoisted to the moor above and two new construction shafts were built. Nearly 2,000 workmen used 120 tons of gelignite to blast the rock away, and the canal tunnel had to be strengthened in places by brick arches. The three railway tunnels are linked by adits into and across headings over the canal tunnel. At Diggle the canal basin had to be abandoned and, because the track of the new railway crossed the canal, a length of canal beyond the original tunnel was covered over with steel girders and a new tunnel mouth built, extending the length of the tunnel to 3 miles 197 yards (5.2km). The first passenger train ran through the tunnel on 5 August 1894.

Trade on the canal had hardly faltered until then, but toll rates were low to remain competitive with the Rochdale Canal. Despite an expenditure of £4,300 the income in 1894 was only £3,441. Trade became increasingly concentrated on the two ends. Only twenty-seven boats passed through Standedge Tunnel that year. Its use was severely disrupted by construction of the new double-track tunnel. Once that was built and there was a four-track railway throughout, the railway company had no real interest in encouraging traffic on the canal or in maintaining the canal.

In fact, the company did maintain the canal, even rebuilding some lock walls in blue engineering brick. Other railways deliberately hindered trade on canals through lack of maintenance or dredging and by lengthy stoppages when maintenance was carried out, seeing

Umbria loaded up ready to sail, above Lock 3W, Stalybridge. *(HCS)*

The new mouth of Standedge Tunnel at Diggle was built when the tunnel was extended to allow the lines to the double-track railway tunnel to pass over the canal. *(HCS)*

The crew of *Reliance* posed for the camera at Lock 20E, Slaithwaite, having travelled through Standedge Tunnel from Stalybridge. *(David Finnis collection)*

their canals as an unnecessary duplication of facilities. Parliament was forced to remind them that they inherited the liabilities of the canal companies and the public right of navigation. Section 17 of the Regulation of Railways Act in 1873 required the railway companies to maintain canals in good order and keep them navigable 'without any unnecessary hindrance, interruption or delay.' This certainly kept some canals open while railways were profitable and may have influenced the LNWR in maintaining the Huddersfield Canal. Less profitable canals not in railway ownership were beginning to close. The Stamford Canal saw its last traffic lost to the railway in 1863 and was soon abandoned. The Wey & Arun Junction Canal was closed in 1868 only three years after a competing railway opened between Horsham and Guildford. By the end of the century through traffic on the Huddersfield Narrow Canal had, to all intents

The railway company maintained the canal at least until the end of the nineteenth century. This lock wall in Marsden was rebuilt in 1895. *(David Finnis collection)*

and purposes, ended. There was virtually no traffic through the tunnel apart from the occasional maintenance boat. The remaining traffic was concentrated at the two ends.

The canal was dying but its effect on the host communities in the Tame and Colne valleys had been immeasurable. In the period between the Duke of Bridgewater building his canal and the railway coming to the valleys, Britain was transformed. It became the workshop of the world, the first country to witness the huge growth of the industrial revolution. The Tame and Colne valleys were in the forefront. The canal, and new turnpike roads, revolutionised transport. The economic and reliable import of raw materials and export of finished goods encouraged rapid growth of the textile industry and investment in new technology, including the changeover from water to steam power.

Industry was drawn to the canal. North End and River Meadow Mills, Stalybridge, in 1893. *(Tameside Local Studies Library)*

The valley settlements had been little more than hamlets with the woollen textile industry in the hands of yeoman clothiers. By the time the railway arrived larger businesses altogether flourished, including cotton mills in the Tame Valley. The cotton industry was totally based in the mill. In the woollen industry large spinning mills were built from the 1820s onward when powered spinning mules were adopted. Handloom weaving remained a home-based industry, although it would not hold out for long against power looms in the mill. In 1839 the Factory Inspectors reported that there were fifty-seven woollen mills and thirty-nine cotton mills in Saddleworth alone. Royal George Mills alongside the canal at Greenfield was opened in 1833. Low Westwood Mill was built as a fulling and carding mill by James Shaw in 1798 at Linthwaite with a loading bay to the canal, and John Crowther started in business with carding engines and spinning mules at nearby Lees Mill in 1840. His sons transformed the business and employed thousands of people. Platts of Dobcross built their famous Dobcross loom works alongside the Diggle locks where supplies of coal could easily be obtained to power the works.

The character of the landscape was changing, not only by the building of the new mills – most of which were very small affairs compared to what would be built in the fifty years after the arrival of the railway – but with the development of a more urban settlement form. Mossley, Greenfield, Uppermill, Dobcross and Diggle in the Tame Valley all became industrial villages with wharves, mills, workers housing and shops, and the same pattern could be seen in the Colne Valley settlements of Marsden, Slaithwaite, Linthwaite, Golcar and Milnsbridge.

Huddersfield had a population of 9,671 in 1811. By 1841 the town had 25,068 people. The Parish Church, The George Inn, and the Cloth Hall were the only large buildings in pre-canal Huddersfield. When the railway arrived, Huddersfield was described in 1844 by Friedrich Engels in his book *The Condition of the Working Class* as 'the handsomest by far of all the factory towns of Yorkshire and Lancashire'. Note, not just that it was handsome (it still has more listed buildings than any provincial town or city in England except Bath), but that it was an industrial town. There was a post office and five banks around the Market Place; there were shops in New Street, King Street and the Market Place. The County Court was built in 1825 and a new and grander Parish Church in 1836. There were mail coaches to

Huddersfield – 'the handsomest by far of all the factory towns of Yorkshire and Lancashire' – in a print by G.D. Tomlinson dated 1837. *(Kirklees Cultural Services)*

Like Huddersfield, Ashton-under-Lyne became a prosperous town. This print by Harwood and Watkins captures Stamford Street with St Peter's Church in 1839. *(Tameside Local Studies Library)*

London, Wakefield, Leeds, Halifax and Manchester, and the streets were lit by gas. Ashton mirrored that growth, from a population of 6,391 in 1801 to 22,678 in 1841. In 1843 there were thirty steam-powered cotton mills in the town. There were also twenty-four cotton mills in Stalybridge whose growth, dependent on the canal for the delivery of coal to power the mills, was even more dramatic. A village of 1,100 people in 1801 had become a busy town of 18,141 people by 1841.

4 Decline, Decay & Vandalism

At the beginning of the twentieth century the Huddersfield Narrow Canal was dead as a through route. The railway was four-tracked. Local goods trains collected and delivered at the stations. Coal trains delivered to merchants in the station yards. The canal was no longer needed, but for canalside premises the narrow boat had the advantage of immediate access without carrying bulky goods from the station. Some trade remained – deliveries of coal in Ashton-under-Lyne, Stalybridge, Mossley, Huddersfield and Milnsbridge – but by 1905 the tonnage carried had fallen to 97,939 tons. The canal was operating at a loss but legally the LNWR had to maintain it. Even the tunnel had to be kept open to provide a water flow to the Ashton and Peak Forest Canals which, after several railway amalgamations, were owned by the Great Central Railway.

The late Victorian era had been a time of stability but change was in the air. The first motors were on the roads and aeroplanes made tentative hops into the air, but Britain was no longer dominant in world trade. Germany was producing more iron and steel and threatening naval supremacy, and the United States was by far the largest economy in terms of market size and output. The country would soon be engulfed in the tragedy of the First World War. In 1916, during the stalemate of that dreadful calamity, a cargo of vitriol substitute was delivered by narrow boat to Messrs R. Radcliffe & Son, Woollen Manufacturers, in Mossley. This was such a rare event that *The Oldham Chronicle* for 8 April noted it as the first working boat through Standedge Tunnel for two and half years.

After the war the world changed completely. There was a new world of radio, Hollywood, and the City. The motor vehicle would end canal carrying as an important means of transport

Slaithwaite coal merchant Sykes's narrow boat *Melville* delivering coal to Cellar's Clough Mill, Marsden in 1910. (David Finnis collection)

London & North Western Railway Maintenance boat, No.2, at Marsden. *(David Finnis collection)*

except on waterways like the Aire & Calder where large barges remained an economic proposition. The economic life of the country was turned upside down. It was more profitable to sell insurance or vacuum cleaners than to weave cloth. New light industrial estates proliferated in the south-east of the country while the old heavy industries of the North and the Midlands began a slow decline. They could not compete with competition from new, more flexible traders abroad; they had not invested sufficiently in modern plant and were slow in appreciating that the world had changed.

This new world was a motorised one. The internal combustion engine was king. Roads were the future – not rails and certainly not the dirty old canals. Soldiers returning from the war found there were no jobs for heroes. The military had given many of them new skills, and the motor vehicle had become a reliable workhorse, albeit needing frequent maintenance and sometimes temperamental. The government sold off around 20,000 surplus trucks cheaply to dealers, who sold them on with easy purchase terms. They were a lifeline to unemployed men with mechanical skills or the administrative skills learned in the forces to control a fleet of vehicles. Regulations were few and far between – as late as 1933 Bedford advertised the WT truck as 'the truck for the 50% overload.' The motor lorry could deliver from door to door. With no limit to the hours worked, little traffic on the roads and the roads free to use – maintained by ratepayers and taxpayers – these small hauliers could not be undercut by the railways or the canal carriers. Soon the small man with one truck became the big concern with many. A new transport system was created almost overnight that was flexible, cheap and convenient. The railway companies struggled to make ends meet. Canal carrying received an ultimately fatal blow.

The internal combustion engine could also power canal boats. As early as 1911 Cadbury's, the chocolate makers, who had a fleet of narrow boats carrying milk and chocolate crumb between dairies and the factory at Bournville, had two boats built with the Swedish Bolinder semi-diesel engine. This crude but reliable and simple engine was ideal for narrow boat use. The chug of the Bolinder and, later, the National and Petter diesels became the sound we associate with the traditional working narrow boat. The traditional boats we see on our canals today, with a motor boat towing a butty, are relics of this last rather sad era of canal carrying. The single boat towed by a horse is much more representative of the real canal age.

The Government had brought the railways under its control during the war and, with them, most of the canals. After the war something had to be done; wartime traffic and lack of maintenance meant that heavy expenditure was needed, but the railways were not as profitable as they had been. The railways were brought together into four big groups in 1923. And with them came the railway-owned canals. The Huddersfield Narrow Canal fell into the ownership of the London, Midland & Scottish Railway (LMS) while its neighbours, the Ashton and Peak Forest Canals, went to the London & North Eastern Railway (LNER).

In 1921, shortly before the grouping of the railways, a cargo of nitre cake was carried from a chemical works near Dewsbury on the *Maid of the Mist* to Mossley. Entering Standedge Tunnel at 2.30 p.m. on 6 November and leaving it at 6.00 p.m. that evening, it was the last working boat through the tunnel.

The canal continued to operate as two separate parts even though the tunnel was dead – but parts whose trade was increasingly limited and unsure. Only 33,000 tons were carried in 1922. By 1938 the railway received £5,504 in tolls and spent £7,404 on maintenance to carry a measly 16,304 tons. They were no longer maintaining the canal. No matter what obligations Parliament placed on them as owners of canals the railways now had no money to invest in the canals. Their pockets were empty. The golden age of steam railways was tarnished. There were celebrated trains like Gresley's A4 streamliners but the core freight and local passenger services had been decimated by road transport and the railway companies struggled to stay in the black. The Great Western Railway would have abandoned the Kennet & Avon Canal in the 1920s had they been able to give it away. The Thames & Severn Canal was not so lucky. Most of it was closed in 1927 and the rest soon followed. The St Helens Canal was historically important in its pre-dating the Bridgewater, but most of it was abandoned in 1931. Traffic had ended on the Stratford Canal and the Union Canal in Scotland by 1933 and the last working boat crossed the summit of the Rochdale in 1937.

The railways now had little time for their canals but the LMS Railway, the owner of the Huddersfield Narrow, had occasion to remember that canals were its responsibility in 1936 when two breaches occurred on canals in their ownership. The Manchester, Bolton & Bury Canal burst its bank at Prestolee and the Shropshire Union Canal suffered a breach near Frankton, on the branch to Llanymynech that we now know as the Montgomery Canal. Neither breach was repaired. Trade on the Huddersfield Narrow and other canals in the company's ownership had effectively finished and the hard-pressed railway saw no future in canals.

With the coming of the Second World War the railways were again brought under government control and, with them, the majority of canals, but the LMS railway decided to cut its losses. Having dipped its toe in the water in 1941 by obtaining powers to close part of the breached Manchester, Bolton & Bury Canal, it presented a Bill to Parliament in 1943 seeking authority to abandon 175 miles of its canals where trade had ended. Amongst those listed was the Huddersfield Narrow Canal, together with large parts of the Shropshire Union network (including the Montgomery Canal and the Newport Branch), most of the Cromford Canal, part of the Ashby Canal and the Caldon Canal. That same year the railway company sold the Huddersfield Broad Canal to the Calder & Hebble Navigation together with the first half mile of the Narrow Canal in Huddersfield up to Chapel Hill bridge. That was the only part of the canal where any trade at all remained, and that very limited. During wartime there was no opposition to the closing of the canals, and on 21 December 1944 the London Midland and Scottish Railway (Canals) Act was approved by Parliament authorising the abandonment of the canals.

The Huddersfield Narrow Canal had been legally abandoned and the public right of navigation extinguished in the first act of official vandalism to affect the canal. It might be closed to boats, but it remained. Its owners had to provide a water flow to the Ashton and Peak Forest Canals and maintain the canal as part of the drainage system without flooding adjoining land, but the railway company no longer had any legal interest in keeping navigational structures in order or preventing the canal from becoming increasingly derelict and unkempt.

5 The IWA Years

The canal was closed but Tunnel End saw more activity than for many a year. The Duke of Wellington's Regiment had a wartime post there to protect the railway tunnel. Possibly the guards lined the canal bank when a party from woollen textile firm W&E Crowther of Slaithwaite had a trip through the tunnel on 14 October 1944, or when members of the Huddersfield Engineering Society were 'legged' through about the same time. These trips marked the beginning of a change of attitude, at first among a very small number of people, but eventually leading to a massive shift in public opinion. The canals were not obsolete, dirty, rubbish-filled ditches; they were historic, had beauty and a special charm that should be cherished.

In the vanguard of this change was an engineer working for the Ministry of Supply. Tom Rolt and his wife Angela spent most of the war years living on *Cressy,* a narrow boat moored on the Worcester & Birmingham Canal. His book *Narrow Boat* had just been published. It tells of how for ten years he planned a journey around the canal system, and when the opportunity came to buy *Cressy,* a Shropshire Union flyboat fitted with a Ford 'Model T' petrol engine with the hold converted to living space, he jumped at the chance. He refitted the cabin at Tooley's boatyard in Banbury, even finding a small bath to fit which was delivered by three men on a handcart from the plumbers' merchants. From the summer of 1939 through to spring 1940 the Rolts travelled slowly (albeit interrupted by Tom taking time off to work because of the onset of the war) through the Midlands canals. *Narrow Boat* has wonderfully evocative descriptions of places they visited, boat people they met, and craft industrial processes they saw – brewing at Allsop's in Burton-on-Trent, bell founding in Loughborough, or the potteries of Stoke-on-Trent. He was describing the end of an era. Tooley's boatyard now only did repair work. A lock-keeper on the Staffordshire & Worcestershire Canal said they were the first boat in six months. There were many places they could no longer reach – the Montgomery, the Wiltshire & Berkshire or the Thames & Severn Canals – and the Kennet & Avon and the Stratford Canals were threatened with closure. Rolt received an avalanche of supporting letters, one from Robert Aickman a literary agent. In the summer of 1945 Aickman and his wife Ray met the Rolts on board *Cressy.* They agreed to form a voluntary body to campaign for the waterways. The following February a meeting took place at the Aickman's home in Gower Street in the Bloomsbury area of London. Robert Aickman was appointed Chairman and Tom Rolt as Secretary. A stranger knocked on the door. 'Is this the meeting of the Inland Waterways Association?' he asked, giving the association its name.

The damage caused by heavy trains on the railways with inadequate maintenance during the war was severe. The railway companies were practically insolvent – or soon would be. With a Labour Government in power the railways were nationalised in 1948. The railway-owned waterways came with them and, in fact, most waterways except the Manchester Ship Canal and its subsidiary the Bridgewater Canal or non-railway canals thought unlikely to be used for carrying again including the Rochdale Canal. The waterways, the railways and parts of the road haulage and bus industries came under the control of the British Transport Commission. In those austere years, with food, clothing and petrol only slowly coming off rationing and the pound being devalued by 30.5% in 1949, public expenditure was tightly controlled. The British Transport Commission was mainly concerned with the railways –

terribly difficult to sort out after losing the pre-war battle with the road hauliers, and too expensive for the impoverished country to resolve – and the canals were lumped together in the Docks & Inland Waterways Executive (DIWE) of the Commission. The DIWE saw its role as being to keep the maintenance bills down. Apart from exceptions such as the Aire & Calder that fitted into the institutional mindset by taking trade to and from the docks, on no account were they going to seriously consider the canals. That might embarrass their political masters and cost money that the country did not have.

The infant Inland Waterways Association (IWA) set about the DIWE with considerable vigour. Aickman became a master political lobbyist using his contacts in the arts world to lobby MPs to fight the waterways corner. There was a series of campaign cruises – 'canal busting' as it was called – beginning on the north Stratford Canal in May 1947. That was obstructed by a low bridge across the canal at Kings Norton, but legally the canal was still open. Rolt took *Cressy* along the canal. The authorities had no choice but to jack up the steel bridge to let him pass. Aickman ensured that the press were there to photograph the event.

Then in 1948 the Huddersfield Narrow hit the headlines. Aickman planned a tour of inspection of northern waterways with Elizabeth Jane Howard, the future novelist, who was acting as typist and general factotum to the IWA. James Sutherland, the IWA Treasurer, and his wife Anthea, would accompany them part of the way before James had to return to work. Tom and Angela Rolt would then join the party. A former wooden ships' lifeboat, *Ailsa Craig*, was hired from Stone in Staffordshire to take them up the Trent & Mersey via the Macclesfield, the Peak Forest and the Ashton Canals to Ashton-under-Lyne. From there they would go via the closed Huddersfield Narrow to Huddersfield and on to Wakefield and Leeds, then return to the Trent & Mersey via the Leeds & Liverpool and Bridgewater Canals. The Huddersfield Narrow Canal was closed to navigation but the Act of Closure allowed pleasure craft to be admitted at the discretion of the railway company. In a move they no doubt later regretted, the DIWE, as successor to the LMS railway, agreed to the passage of *Ailsa Craig*. Presumably wishing to placate these awkward individuals, the DIWE even offered a gang of men to help.

All went well until they reached the Peak Forest. That was so overgrown as to be almost impassable and they encountered underwater obstructions including a massive boiler in the arm of the Ashton Canal leading to the Huddersfield Narrow. The promised gang of men was sheltering from pouring rain under a tarpaulin by Lock 1W. The canal was very shallow and they had to be dragged along. *Ailsa Craig* scraped over the bottom all the way between locks 3W and 4W. Then the inevitable happened. As the boat rose in lock 4W water flooded in through a hole torn in the hull by the rough treatment. The boat began to sink. Somehow the gang got the boat out of the lock and drained the canal. They were stuck on the bottom of a rapidly drying canal in the pouring rain in a strange northern town that they did not even know the name of. They thought they were in Ashton (the story of their exploits was written about or told that way) but actually they were in Stalybridge. Lock 4W is near the centre of that small town. The mills downstream that took in water from the canal had to stop production as the water dried up. A letter was immediately sent to Sir Reginald Hill, Chairman of the DIWE. And, no doubt, the mill owners were also seeking action. Two days later Wilf Donkersley, the local canal superintendent, appeared with two shipwrights. They quickly repaired the rent in the hull and *Ailsa Craig* was under way again guided now by Wilf. They made it to Diggle, where the Rolts joined them, and even through Standedge Tunnel – though not without drama. As they followed the canal maintenance boat through the tunnel, *Ailsa Craig* jammed in the narrow bore. Elizabeth Jane Howard, who was steering, managed to reverse clear and by prizing the wooden rubbing strips off the fragile hull, they got through. At Marsden they were black from soot deposited on the tunnel walls by steam engine smoke, and caught a train to Huddersfield. The George Hotel provided a bath and a meal.

The trip was a huge success in publicising the plight of the canals, but the DIWE had been put to a lot of trouble, embarrassment and expense. Not long afterwards lockgates were removed and the process of putting concrete cascades into the locks soon followed.

Ailsa Craig on the way to the Huddersfield Narrow. Elizabeth Jane Howard (steering) and Anthea Sutherland, with Robert Aickman ready to jump ashore to work one of the Trent and Mersey Canal locks. *(James Sutherland)*

Tours of inspection were a great adventure, but the IWA had a serious task: to save the waterways. They were faced by totally unimaginative officialdom that saw the canals as long past their use-by-date and its prime role as the guardian of an impoverished public purse. The threat to the waterways was very real and could have been fatal. Not just the peripheral canals or ones already closed such as the Huddersfield Narrow, the very core of the system came under threat of closure. At first the threat was of closure by stealth through a lack of maintenance but, as the DIWE desperately tried to balance the books, it sought to legally close more and more canals in a desperate attempt to stem the losses. The waterways were seen as an outdated transport system. No other benefits – as part of the drainage system, as a leisure resource, or environmental and aesthetic – were considered. No thought was given to the future cost of putting right the problems caused by a lack of maintenance. Abandoned canals became an eyesore and a danger to children. As they silted up they would not even function properly as drainage channels.

The IWA had a mountain to climb. But climb it they did and twenty years later they had won the major battle – if not the war. The 1968 Transport Act marked the end of officialdom's attempt to close the system. Waterways were to be divided into three categories. Commercial Waterways such as the Aire & Calder were essentially broad waterways linked to the docks. Cruising Waterways were the main network of canals centred mainly in the Midlands that was being used increasingly for pleasure boating – for the first time government recognised a purpose for the canals in addition to the carriage of goods. Finally came an awfully long list of canals described as the Remainder. These remainder waterways, including the Huddersfield Narrow, were, in effect, to be left to their own devices. The Act specified that they would be maintained to the minimum standard required for public safety and amenity, but amenity counted for little to the bean-counters of Whitehall. Much to the dismay of the IWA the Act abolished the statutory public rights of navigation contained in the various Canal Acts and railway legislation. They had been able to use these as a trump card proving by 'canal busting' exploits that statutory rights were being exercised by the public.

On the face of it the Act did not seem much of a success, and the loss of rights of navigation outweighed any benefits, but Barbara Castle, the Minister responsible, saw the Act as a monument to her determination to overcome civil service inertia and a vital step in the acceptance by government that the waterways had a new and brighter future. Control of the nationalised waterways had been divorced from the docks, the railways and buses in 1963 when an independent statutory body, the British Waterways Board (BW), was set up. After the 1968 Act BW no longer had the stomach to propose further canals for closure. The whole process had been very damaging and the political brickbats orchestrated by the IWA were not popular with their political masters. The act provided a shelter for inactivity by giving BW a period of grace to consider the options and, for the first time, the possibility that a waterway might be restored was accepted. BW was also allowed to work in partnership with local authorities and even voluntary societies to achieve that aim.

It had taken twenty years to get to this point but the battles in and out of Parliament, and to refute the recommendations of official reports that would have seen the bulk of the canal system abandoned, had been hard fought. There had been casualties. Only about half of the once flourishing waterways remained navigable. The Huddersfield Narrow's neighbours had not fared well. The Barnsley, the Dearne & Dove, the Manchester, Bolton & Bury and the Rochdale Canals had all been abandoned – apart from a short length of the Rochdale in Manchester – and most of the Chesterfield Canal. The final part of the historic St Helens that remained after the closure of the rest in 1931 and the locks at Runcorn linking the Bridgewater Canal to the Mersey were closed too. There had also been casualties within the IWA. When the first of the very successful National Rallies was held at Market Harborough in 1950 *Cressy* was relegated to a remote mooring. Tom Rolt had been unable to work with Robert Aickman. He went on to form the Talyllyn Railway Preservation Society, the first railway preservation society – thus laying the foundations not only of the waterways movement but also of the heritage railway movement – before leaving that to concentrate on earning his living through his books.

A movement to restore lost waterways was well underway by the time of the 1968 Act. As early as 1950 Douglas Barwell set up a non-profit making charitable trust which purchased the navigation rights of the Lower Avon Navigation for £1,500. The locks and weirs on the river were restored using voluntary labour with help from the Royal Engineers, and contractors such as the Trust raised the money and by 1962 the river navigation was again open from Evesham to Tewkesbury. Not only was this the first waterway restoration scheme to be completed, it showed the way forward by a local group. The IWA had saved the waterways nationally. It would be local groups that would save individual waterways. The Kennet & Avon Canal Association was formed shortly after the Lower Avon Navigation Trust but it was not until 1963, after petitions to Parliament and a battle to prevent the legal closure of the unnavigable canal, that British Waterways agreed to spend part of its maintenance expenditure on restoration of the canal while the Kennet & Avon Canal Trust (as the Association had become) raised funds and provided volunteers. The canal eventually re-opened in 1990. And by 1968 the Stratford Canal had re-opened, this time under the temporary aegis of the National Trust, in a project managed by the energetic David Hutchings who gave up his architectural career to see the canal officially re-opened by HM the Queen Mother on 11 July 1964. His technique of using volunteers, the army and prisoners was successful where the main cost was labour, but would not restore the Huddersfield Narrow Canal in the condition it was now in.

While our attention has been diverted to the national picture, terrible things had happened to the Huddersfield Narrow. By 1968 it was no longer a canal, but a series of disconnected pounds, some holding water, others apparently full of rubbish. Sections had been filled in or

No boats could pass this way. The overgrown canal above Lock 1W, Ashton-under-Lyne. *(HCS)*

Rubbish in the canal, and the cascaded Lock 3W, Stalybridge. *(Kathryn Gibson)*

built over, and bridges lowered. In 1951 the top gates of the locks were removed to be replaced by a concrete weir. Then over a period of time – and not completed until the 1970s – most of the lock chambers were filled with rubble or the sides bulldozed into the lock chamber, and then concreted over to form a cascade which soon became unsightly, as the concrete cracked when the supporting rubble settled. A few locks were simply capped over with reinforced concrete that supported a layer of soil and scrubby grass.

The short length in Huddersfield transferred to the Calder & Hebble Navigation in 1944 and the arm of the Broad Canal connecting that to Aspley Basin were closed by a further Act of Parliament in 1962. No boats had reached Huddersfield for eight years on the Broad Canal until May 1961 when a small flotilla led by Lionel Munk, Chairman of the IWA, and Robert Aickman moored in Aspley Basin. In January 1962 the IWA brought eight boats up to Huddersfield led by West Country keel *Pauline* to deliver a petition against the closure, but the council saw no future in waterways and filled in the canal where it was crossed by the main Wakefield Road. That was cheaper than building a new six-lane highway bridge. The Huddersfield Narrow was cut-off from Aspley Basin and the canal network as part of the town's plans for dealing with motor traffic.

After passing through two locks and under Queen Street South bridge the canal, was again filled in. BW had sold off a few yards for textile manufacturer Bates & Co. to extend their premises with a yard by the roadside and a new shed beyond, built between their traditional mill buildings on each side of the canal. Then, beyond Chapel Hill, a longer length that

The factory of Bates & Co. built
across the canal in Huddersfield.
(Derek Walker)

included the wharf and warehouses at Engine Bridge, had passed into the ownership of Sellers
Engineers to build an extension of their textile machinery factory, with a short length beyond
that sold to the textile mill of Haigh & Co.

Further up the Colne Valley the Urban District Council had filled in the canal through the
centre of Slaithwaite with the water culverted in a pipe. Instead of the canal there was now a
footpath, a car park and a pleasant grassed area bordered by cherry trees. The main road bridge
was lowered to avoid the hump of the old canal bridge.

In the Tame Valley nearly a quarter of a mile of the canal was filled in alongside Hartshead
power station, but the worst destruction was in Stalybridge where the canal had been
obliterated through the town centre. Armentières Square was a car park, and the Castle Hall
Sports Centre encroached on the canal close to the spot where *Ailsa Craig* had been
marooned. Delta Cables, one of the largest employers in the district, and the Millwood
Rubber Co. both had factory buildings or yards on the line of the canal.

And that was not all. Individual bridges had been lowered or culverted at Stoney Battery
and Lees Mill in the Colne Valley where the main road bridge into Milnsbridge had also been
widened with a prop in the canal bed, blocking the tail of a lock. Wool Road bridge,
Dobcross, and High Street bridge, Uppermill, were both obliterated and at Wool Road the
canal had been filled in to allow the road to be widened. Frenches Bridge and Manns Wharf
bridge in Greenfield had been replaced by culvert pipes to take the water and the swing-
bridge for the minor Grove Road further down the valley replaced by a fixed bridge just
above water level. These were not the only problem bridges either. When the canal was filled
in through Slaithwaite and Stalybridge the local authorities had seized the opportunity to
remove or replace other humped or horse and cart weight-limited bridges. A total of eighteen

Slaithwaite in 1956. Contractors working
for the Colne Valley Urban District
Council laying a pipe culvert along the
bed of the canal to carry the water prior to
filling in the canal.
(David Finnis collection)

road bridges would have to be replaced or substantially rebuilt if boats were ever again to
navigate the canal. Several pipes crossed the canal just above water level and a main sewer
below Lock 1W embedded in concrete at water level prevented access to the canal.

The links to the main system via the Ashton and Peak Forest Canals were no longer
navigable. The Rochdale Canal locks in Manchester were in such a bad state that members
of the IWA took twelve days to take the narrow boat *Parrot* up the locks to the junction with
the Ashton Canal in 1964. The Rochdale Canal Co.'s neglect of these locks was trivial
compared to BW's lack of maintenance on the Ashton and Peak Forest Canals. They had no
intention of spending public money on the Peak Forest between Marple locks and Portland
Basin, or the Ashton from there to Manchester. Both branches of the Ashton Canal were
legally abandoned in 1961, but BW had no right to prevent navigation of the main line of
that canal or the Peak Forest Canal. Apart from severing the link to the Huddersfield Narrow,
that would close the Cheshire Ring of Canals. Eight boats took part in a cruise organised by
the IWA to publicise the situation in 1961. Only one completed the journey from Marple to
Manchester, and that by being lifted out of the canal and dragged around a lock whose gates
had been set on fire and smashed into the bottom of the lock.

In the winter of 1961–62 Outram's magnificent aqueduct over the River Goyt at Marple
on the Peak Forest Canal was damaged by water leaking into the stonework. BW wished to
demolish it at a cost of £7,000 rather than find £35,000 for repairs. The Clerk of the
Bredbury and Romiley Urban District Council (the Goyt forming the boundary between that
District and Marple) called a meeting of local authorities along the line of the canals. They
agreed that the aqueduct was important and the money must be found. BW repaired the
aqueduct, perhaps with a degree of bad grace because the councils had wrong-footed them

Slaithwaite was bad – but Stalybridge was much worse. There was no evidence that a canal had ever passed through the town centre in this 1996 view of Armentières Square. *(Alan Stopher)*

Looking south-west towards Hartshead Power Station. Only a short pound remained in water between blockages. *(HCS)*

by getting it scheduled as an Ancient Monument, preventing demolition. But the locks at Marple were unusable and in 1964 the Peak Forest Canal Society was formed. The Society began regular working parties on the canal. BW refused permission for them to work on the locks but they were deteriorating fast. The Society moved the working parties there, making no secret of their action, gaining maximum publicity and defying BW to stop them. BW then blocked off the aqueduct at Store Street in Manchester on the Ashton Canal after a minor leak and took the water across the aqueduct in pipes. The volunteers continued repairing the canal. Locks were cleared of rubbish and repointed; broken lock gates were repaired with secondhand timber. Volunteers were working on other canals too – the Basingstoke, the Droitwich and the Montgomery – which brings us back to 1968.

Graham Palmer of the London branch of the IWA had been producing *Navvies Notebook* recording local canal groups and details of working parties. This venture became the Waterway Recovery Group, a national volunteer co-ordination group that still exists as a subsidiary of the IWA, holding work camps throughput the country. In conjunction with the Peak Forest Canal Society, he planned a massive operation, Operation Ashton, to take place in September 1968 bringing volunteers to the Ashton Canal from all over the country. The Ashton was in such a sorry state that local residents and the councils could see no option but to fill the canal in, but it is not easy to dispose of a canal. The water supply has to be diverted and the land drainage functions replaced by pipes, culverts or new water channels. As early as 1961 BW knew that to fill in the canal would cost £3 million; no doubt it would have cost more by 1968. With nobody in sight who might pay that, BW took the line of least resistance and helped the volunteers by draining the canal and making sure their staff were around. Over 600 volunteers turned up and the organisation was there to support them. Food and places to sleep were provided, together with dumpers and trucks to cart away the 2,000 tons of rubbish cleared from the canal, and canal washwalls and copings were repaired. There was much to do and the Ashton locks to repair, but Operation Ashton had a huge impact.

BW had a vigorous chairman in Sir Frank Price. He brought the local authorities along the line of both canals together and a formula was agreed to restore the canals with the costs shared. The IWA raised £10,000 towards the Ashton Canal and the Peak Forest Canal Society £3,000 towards the Peak Forest Canal plus the continued work of their volunteers. One of the hardest tasks was to dredge the top pound of the Ashton Canal in the Portland Basin area. Access was poor and, as *Ailsa Craig* found more than twenty years earlier, there were large objects dumped in the canal. So, in a groundbreaking collaboration with British Waterways, Graham Palmer organised Ashtac for a weekend in March 1972. The canal was drained and as many as 1,000 volunteers removed 3,000 tons of accumulated debris. When the volunteers left, BW continued work and on 13 May 1974 the Minister, David Howells, unveiled a plaque alongside the canal at Vesta Street, Manchester to officially re-open the canals.

In fact 1974 was a good year for re-openings. Further south, seventeen and a half miles of the Caldon Canal were re-opened with local authority help and the Upper Avon Navigation, that connected the Lower Avon at Evesham with the Stratford Canal in Stratford – both already restored – was officially re-opened by the Queen Mother.

Grove Road, crossing the canal between Mossley and Stalybridge – one of many lowered or culverted bridges, and only a minor road! The much larger Wakefield Road in Huddersfield carried six lanes of traffic. *(HCS)*

6 A Pennine Dream (2)

In autumn 1972 Bob Dewey, a young chartered town planner, moved north to take up a new job. He walked the towpath of the Huddersfield Narrow Canal and, for the first time, saw the mouth of Standedge Tunnel. He bombarded Margaret Sinfield, the Chairman of the IWA West Riding Branch, with letters and phone calls about the canal. Together with John Maynard, a colleague on the Branch Committee, she arranged a meeting on *Elizabeth B*, a West Country keel converted to a club room that was moored in Aspley Basin. About a dozen people attended. Bob Dewey spread Ordnance Survey maps around. His enthusiasm convinced them that the canal must be restored. A smaller meeting between Margaret Sinfield, John Maynard, Bob Dewey and Ralph Kirkham (the Chairman of the Calder Navigation Society) was arranged to discuss ways and means. They decided to form a society to promote restoration of the canal. A public meeting would be arranged to launch the Huddersfield Canal Society (soon to be universally known as HCS) with John Maynard as Chairman and Bob Dewey as Secretary.

The meeting was held on the evening of 19 April 1974 at the Zetland Hotel in Huddersfield (now O'Neil's). The fifty-two people present were a mixture of local people, IWA members and Peak Forest Canal Society members. A Committee was elected and a set of rules adopted. The initial enthusiasm was soon dampened. Bob Dewey wrote to tell BW that the Society had been formed. Mr A.J. Brawn, the Chief Estates Officer, replied that the canal was 'being made safe by capping locks.' There could be 'no question of restoring this canal.' The message came across loud and clear. It was not going to be easy, but the Committee knew that the Ashton and the Peak Forest had been restored after regular working parties and the 'Big Dig' of Operation Ashton. That surely was the way forward. To have regular volunteer working parties on the canal was the priority. But the first generation restoration projects had been on waterways that were generally intact if the locks and other features could be put into working order. Interest was now turning to waterways that would cost millions of pounds to restore. Of these second generation projects the Huddersfield Narrow was probably the most difficult with seventy-four locks to restore, a three and a quarter mile long tunnel, and one and a half miles of the canal completely obliterated and even built on. Officialdom doubted the sanity of these people. They clearly had an impossible dream – more so, perhaps, than that of the original promoters of the canal.

The first thing to do was to increase membership. The more members there were, the more the Society would be listened to and the more bodies would be available for the all-important working parties. Regular bulletins were issued, duplicated on a borrowed Gestetner machine that John Maynard thought had a mind of its own. An exhibition was produced and taken to waterway events, towpath walks were organised, and slide shows given of the canal and restoration work.

BW had no enthusiasm for working parties. They blamed the unions who were concerned that volunteers would take work from their members, but the fundamental issue was that a restored canal would cost more to maintain. Legally they could only spend what was necessary to maintain the canal as a remainder waterway. Their response to requests to work on the canal was a deafening silence. There was no question of defying BW and working without permission as on the Peak Forest. None of the Huddersfield locks could be cleared of silt and patched up; the concrete cascades and rubble infill had to be cleared out; most would need at least a partial rebuild of the walls; and they all needed new lockgates and paddle gear. The Society had £40 in the bank.

In his typical dry manner, John Maynard said the first year was 'not a complete disaster' and warned members not to become discouraged. In fact the Society had laid stronger foundations than was apparent. Over 160 members might not sound many – but few small voluntary groups achieve that substance within their first year. The Society was solvent and behind the scenes work was going on to produce a feasibility study showing that the canal could be restored. This was the work of several committee members – Chris Griffiths, Alan West, Bob Dewey and Brian Beagley – Bob Keaveney and fellow Peak Forest Canal Society member David Brown had earlier surveyed the canal. *The Huddersfield Narrow Canal – a unique waterway: A preliminary survey of the feasibility and desirability of its restoration* was produced to the standard of, for example, reports then produced by local authority departments. Waterway restoration was said to have 'attained respectability.' The canal could form a linear park along a potential 'corridor of leisure' joining Greater Manchester and West Yorkshire. Crucially the conclusion was that there were no problems that could not be overcome by modern engineering methods. The meat of the report took the form of a series of maps showing the situation along the canal – which locks were capped over, which were part demolished and cascaded, or which were cascaded within an undamaged lock chamber; which parts of the canal were infilled, and identifying buildings on the line.

The study was launched at a boat rally at Portland Basin to celebrate the re-opening of the Ashton and Peak Forest Canals in June 1975. Copies were sent to the local authorities. After the reorganisation of 1974 these were the Metropolitan Counties of Greater Manchester and West Yorkshire, and the Metropolitan Districts of Tameside (Ashton, Stalybridge and Mossley), Oldham (the Saddleworth area between Greenfield and Diggle) and Kirklees (the Colne Valley). BW, councillors, MPs and anyone who may influence decision makers received a copy, including the Inland Waterways Amenity Advisory Council (IWAAC). Set up by the 1968 Transport Act to advise government and the Waterways Board, IWAAC was chaired by John Barratt. He had been the County Planning Officer in Staffordshire before the 1974 reorganisation (and coincidentally my boss there) and had been involved in bringing the Caldon Canal back into use. Impressed by the study, he gave the Society its first official recognition. IWAAC members visited the canal in October 1975. They considered the study to be a professional document, although acknowledging that more work was needed to find a solution for the infilled canal through Stalybridge. IWAAC recommended that BW and the local authorities should adopt a policy that the canal should be protected from further development or infilling.

This was the most important first task for HCS. Destruction was still continuing. The last locks were being cascaded at Royal George in Greenfield. The local authorities had to be persuaded to adopt suitable planning policies. The first generation of local authority-produced plans were out of date. Councils in the Metropolitan County areas were developing their second generation plans – Structure Plans setting out broad policies for the county with more detailed Local Plans being produced by each district council. It was essential that these new plans included policies preventing further development on the canal and that a route was protected from end-to-end. Councils were making decisions based on drafts of their new plans; the sooner they adopted draft policies to protect the canal route from further encroachment the better.

Society members lobbied councillors and the leaders of the councils and key chief officers; indeed from this time onwards most of these people were known to the Society. All of them were added to a growing list of influential people who received free copies of the members bulletin that was now appearing on a bi-monthly basis, and had been given the very appropriate name *Pennine Link* (unofficially shortened to 'Plink'). The combination of lobbying, the professionalism of the feasibility study and the support of IWAAC led to all of the local authorities, with Greater Manchester in the lead followed by Kirklees, soon adopting non-encroachment policies, although in Tameside the route through Stalybridge remained unresolved. The Society's timing could not have been better. Not only did it fit into the local authorities' timetables for reviewing their policies, but HCS was knocking at a door that at this moment was ajar. The local authorities and the public were increasingly environment conscious; they could appreciate the principle of a green corridor. The once booming economies of the Tame and Colne Valleys based on the textile industries were faltering. Jobs were being lost. All was far from well with the economy nationally. As in the years when the canal was built, inflation was affecting everyone with a rapid loss of purchasing power and higher and higher wage demands to keep up. What else was there for these valleys? New industry was unlikely to go there. Tourism might offer something, at least for the upper parts of the valleys – indeed Uppermill was beginning to attract visitors to walk along the canal or go to the new Saddleworth Museum. Stopping further encroachment on the canal kept the options open and did not commit the councils to paying for future restoration – a key factor as they were strapped for cash with budgets tightly regulated by Whitehall. It was probably just as well that the Society kept to itself that their rough estimate of the total cost of restoration was about £19 million.

The Society was spreading its wings, getting publicity and beginning the slow process of gaining respect. Not only was HCS able to sell its feasibility study as a serious document, but it could also sell a stick of Standedge Rock or a cuddly toy in the shape of a 'Diggle'. Peter Freeman, who came on the committee to organise events and publicity, described the Diggles in *Pennine Link* as 'a shy homely race [who] were driven from Scandinavia by the marauding Wegis...[and] eventually came to settle in the natural caverns under...[Standedge].' I never have found out who the marauding Wegis were! So many of these stuffed toys with white or grey furry bodies, a rather large head and pink ears and hands, wearing red waistcoats were sold that a knitting pattern was reproduced in *Pennine Link*.

At last BW had a partial change of heart concerning working parties, with an event on the weekend of 10 and 11 April 1976 organised by committee member Tim Noakes and the Waterway Recovery Group. Three basic tasks were attempted on the canal above Slaithwaite: repairing the towpath, repairing the boundary wall, and cutting back trees between the towpath and the canal. Plant and materials were begged or borrowed mainly from Kirklees Council who even provided a lorry and driver free of charge. Dumpers were borrowed from the Peak Forest Canal Society and the Inland Waterways Protection Society. Volunteers came from far and wide. Huddersfield Voluntary Aid provided tea, soup and beefburgers. Even the weather stayed fine. The result was half a mile of level towpath, invasive vegetation removed and most of the stone wall repaired. A great success and *Pennine Link* announced that the next working party would be on the actual canal channel – but it would be several years before BW would contemplate that possibility.

Just as things were looking better, HCS faced what John Maynard described as its Dunkirk. A planning application was submitted by Bates & Co. to extend their factory in Huddersfield with a new building between Queen Street South and the building that was already on the route of the canal. It would double the length of the obstruction and, realistically, cut off the original route of the canal. Kirklees Council had adopted a policy of protecting the route of the canal but the canal was already filled in here. It was in the ownership of the company and Bates's promised the creation of new jobs – a subject coming to the fore as jobs continued to be lost elsewhere. HCS, individual members and IWAAC objected. The council looked for a compromise but, finding none, granted planning permission on 2 July 1976. A new route for the canal seemed inevitable, possibly by canalising the River Colne – but that was an upland river, subject to dramatic changes in levels and flows.

Only months later a nearby firm, the Eldon Combing Co., submitted another planning application to build a warehouse blocking the canal between Bates's and Chapel Hill. Again objections were made but, in view of another promise to create jobs and the decision on the Bates's application, the worst was expected. Bates's and, on the opposite side of Chapel Hill, Sellers effectively blocked off this part of the canal. Bob Dewey and fellow committee member Derek Walker went out, took some levels and came up with an entirely original solution that was quickly published as *A New Canal for Huddersfield* in December 1976 before the council considered the application. Reconstructing the canal as originally built was dismissed. It would require the destruction of industrial premises. Diverting the canal into and making the River Colne navigable was theoretically possible, but the main road crossing of the obvious link between the canal and the river at Firth Street had insufficient headroom and the road could not be raised. A new solution was needed.

Tunnelling under the major obstacles at Bates's and Sellers was suggested to meet everyone's objective. The existing Lock 2E could be removed, with the water level beyond this under Queen Street South bridge lowered through a new tunnel under the factory. A new Lock 2E could be sited where the tunnel emerged beyond Bates's factory. Similarly the existing Lock 3E could be removed, the canal could be lowered beyond this with a cut-and-cover tunnel through the Sellers site and a new Lock 3E built to the west of that site. The council and the landowners were asked to safeguard this as the preferred route against future development. The report was widely circulated and sent to members of the committee that would decide on the Eldon Combing Co.'s application. To the Society's immense gratitude the council refused permission.

Eldon Combing Co. did not appeal against the refusal, and Bates's showed no signs of actually building their extension. Then in August 1977 Bates's put in another application reducing the size of their approved building. There seemed no likelihood that Kirklees would refuse this and, even if permission was refused, the company could build the original scheme. But objections were made. To everyone's astonishment, especially the council's officers, the planning committee refused the application. Now that a solution to the problem had been found they wanted the new building to be designed from the outset so that it would later be straightforward to put in a tunnel rather than to have to dig up the floor and the foundations – although that would be needed in the older building behind.

To their enormous credit Bates's quickly submitted a new proposal with the ground floor of the building raised to allow for the canal to be built through this part of the site at the lower level suggested by the Society. To ensure this met everyone's requirements the chairman of the planning committee, Councillor George Speight – who was to become a great friend and ally to the Society – asked John Maynard and Bob Dewey to meet planning officers, Mr Bates and his architects so that there could be no misunderstanding. The Society withdrew its objection, offering support to the proposal and planning permission was granted. The downturn in the economy delayed work on the new building but a revised scheme was built in the early 1980s that retained the principle of supporting the building on columns to allow the canal to be threaded through the site.

The partnership of Bob Dewey and Derek Walker turned to look at the options for rebuilding the canal through Stalybridge. *Through Stalybridge by Boat: A study into the alternative ways of restoring the Huddersfield Narrow Canal through Stalybridge* was edited by Peter Freeman and published in December 1977. Rebuilding the canal on the original route would involve significant disruption, especially to the firms who had buildings on the line of the canal. A Huddersfield-type solution, changing the level to slot a canal underneath premises on the original line, could create an attractive landscaped area through the town centre. Pubs and shops would benefit, but it would be very disruptive when work was carried out and delays in the release of land were likely. A third option, referred to as the River Route, created links from the canal at each end of the blockage into the nearby River Tame, which would be made navigable. Possible connecting points and locations of locks in the river were considered. Although navigation would be interrupted during periods of flooding, the line was clear of buildings and there would be no disruptive work in the town centre. The report compared

The new extension to Bates & Co. in Huddersfield, with space underneath to allow the canal to be rebuilt beyond Queen Street Bridge (in the foreground). *(HCS)*

The River Tame in Stalybridge. Would the canal have to be diverted this way? *(HCS)*

the river to towns with attractive waterside frontages, and concluded that this was the most practical route.

HCS had a caravan that had been rebuilt and repainted by working parties arranged by enthusiastic member Ian Stott. It was parked in Stalybridge for the launch of the document. Committee member David Finnis arranged the event beginning his successful career publicising the society. Newspapers, radio, television, councils, councillors, MPs and other interested organisations were sent copies of the report. Radio Manchester interviewed members and local newsagents were supplied with copies for sale. Local people were enthusiastic, with a strong feeling that the canal should never have been filled in.

HCS was making progress – gaining new members, being regularly in the news and gaining respect – but nothing was happening on the canal. Towards the end of 1976 Wells Management Consultants Ltd, a London-based consultancy with expertise in fund-raising, offered help. At the Annual General Meeting the following year it was agreed that they be appointed to advise the Society at a cost of £500, with the aim of setting up a working party between HCS, the local authorities, BW and other interested parties that could lead to the formation of a charitable Trust to organise fund-raising and a restoration programme. An appeal was made for funds and meetings were held but nothing concrete developed. At the 1978 AGM John Maynard had to report that it had not been possible to set up the working party. There was criticism that the Society had spent a great deal of money for very little, but HCS gained in the long-term by the focus placed on the need for a partnership approach and by seeing just how difficult that would be to achieve.

The idea of having a festival to publicise the Society and the canal was discussed at monthly meetings now being held in pubs east and west. Derek Walker took on the task of organising this, with the help of other Society and IWA members and the Huddersfield Sea Scouts. The festival took place on 24 and 25 September 1977 in the car park of the Huddersfield Polytechnic alongside the detached arm of the Huddersfield Broad Canal between Wakefield Road and Lock 1E. The canal here had been owned by the Polytechnic since the major

Boats on the short arm of the Huddersfield Broad Canal leading to the Huddersfield Narrow. Huddersfield Canal Festival, September 1977. *(Derek Walker)*

buildings of the campus were built a few years earlier. More than forty boats – narrow boats, a Calder & Hebble barge, and fibreglass and wooden cruisers – were moored across the road in Aspley Basin or on the Broad Canal. Trail boats were launched alongside the Polytechnic. There were entertainments, displays and exhibitions and widespread press, radio and local television coverage. The Chairman of the West Yorkshire County Council, the Deputy Mayor of Kirklees and all the local MPs were there, as was BW Area Engineer, John Freeman. The Waterway Recovery Group and the Society's volunteers tackled Lock 1E during the weekend, hoping to clear the chamber of rubbish and patch up the lockgates. BW's approval was not required. This lock belonged to the Polytechnic. The working party attracted the attention of the public but was hardly a success; the pump to clear water from the lock chamber was too small to prevent leakage through the lockgates. Small working parties were held through that autumn and the lock was made to look presentable. BW even found a set of paddle gears to replace those which were missing.

Publicity and spreading the word was shown to be vital by the festival. The Councils may be leaning towards the views of the Society, but the Wells episode showed they were far from becoming willing partners. In a short period in the summer of 1977 the caravan was taken to Slaithwaite Carnival, where Diggles were seen in the parade (adult-sized costumes had appeared!), to Colne Valley High School Fete, to Milnsbridge Carnival, to Worsley Boat Show, to Saddleworth Rugby Club, to Oldham Sheep Dog Trials, to the East Pennine Transport Rally in Greenhead Park, Huddersfield, to the Pennine Show at Holmfirth, to Uppermill to recruit members from visitors, to Diggle Show and for a week in September with a display in Huddersfield town centre.

After the success of the first canal festival, a second – the Tameside Canals Festival – was organised for the weekend of 29 and 30 July 1978 with help from the Peak Forest Canal Society and the IWA at Portland Basin. Peter Freeman was chairman and general organiser. Again it was a huge success; the horse-drawn boat *Maria* gave trips along the Ashton Canal; visiting boats were moored on the Peak Forest Canal; CAMRA (the **Cam**pagin for **R**eal **A**le) sold twenty-five barrels of beer; there were exhibits of canal ware, corn dolly making, clog making, and of works by canal artists; and there were brass bands, a pipe band, Morris dancers, children's entertainers, folk singers, a tug-of-war across the canal and a barbecue on the Saturday night. The Mayor officially opened the Festival and received a letter from the Mayor of Kirklees delivered by David Finnis and Don McCallum who had canoed the length of the canal from Huddersfield in two days. MPs Tom Pendry and Robert Sheldon and John Freeman of BW were guests, and local industrialist, Sir George Kenyon was the Festival President. Not only did the Festival focus attention on the canals and the plight of the Huddersfield Narrow, it also raised over £1,000.

Just before the Festival there had been another attempt at clearing the chamber of lock 1E. A temporary causeway across the canal below the lock gave access between different parts of the Polytechnic. Only a makeshift stopper could be made to stop water flow through the culvert in the causeway and the water dropped very little on the Saturday. By midnight the water level was at last going down and it looked as though progress might be possible on Sunday. Then what had been merely tragic became a complete farce. The pump ran out of fuel! By daybreak the water level was back to normal. Nothing more could be done.

New members were coming on to the Committee – Chris Farrar, Trevor Ellis, David Sumner, Les Winnard and Graham Maskell – who would become increasingly important. The new Committee was restive, wanting to make faster progress; meetings were becoming harder to control and on occasions were quite raucous. John Maynard was concerned that members must 'let the other chap have his say.' He felt that he had been Chairman for long enough and Derek Walker was proposed to replace him, but Derek was offered a new job in the Midlands, taking him away from the area.

Change was in the air. HCS had outgrown the way it operated as an informal group of volunteers. Capital was being accrued from successful events, and the Society had hundreds

Working party at Lock 1E during the Canal Festival. Although the lock remained inoperable, the working party was a huge publicity success. No safety fences in those days! *(Derek Walker)*

of members. It had to have more standing and a firmer legal status. John Maynard had been quietly talking to John Freeman, the BW Area Engineer, about Standedge Tunnel. It might not accord with official BW policy, but Standedge Tunnel was special, and the idea of emulating the success of the Dudley Canal Trust who were – indeed still are – running a trip boat into Dudley Tunnel in the Midlands appealed to both Johns. But the cost of repairs to the tunnel, and the health and safety implications, were too much. Consideration had been given to the sort of organisation that could operate tunnel trips. A trust of some kind was suggested and John Fryer, a Huddersfield solicitor, was brought in to advise. He recommended that a tunnel trust should be a limited liability company – limited by guarantee rather than with capital held by shareholders – to protect the interests of members and the ruling committee. There would also be benefits in having charitable status. It was apparent that the benefits of being a limited liability company and a charity applied equally to the Society. So John Fryer was persuaded to join the Committee and arrange for HCS to become a charitable company as thoughts turned towards a more professional approach to the way the Society carried out its business.

The first evidence of this was a superbly simple new logo designed by Clodagh Brown. This has stood the test of time; more than twenty years later it does not look dated – provided it is drawn exactly as designed.

By 1979, when John Maynard stood down as Chairman, he had held that position for five years. Of the original committee members only John and Bob Dewey remained. Some members had resigned for personal or work reasons. Others left because they felt progress was too slow. There was no longer any thought that work by volunteers could shame the authorities into action. That completely misunderstood the scale of the task. The way ahead was far from clear but key things had been achieved. HCS had a large membership, was actively spreading the word and had contacts with all of the local authorities, BW, MPs and with the local press. The Society had plausible plans showing that the canal could physically be restored, but did not yet know how those plans could be realised. Most important, they had saved the canal from further destruction.

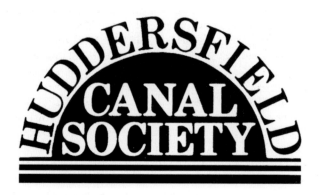

The Huddersfield Canal Society logo designed by Clodagh Brown.

7 A Change of Gear

Chris Farrar, a metallurgist, succeeded John Maynard as Chairman of HCS at the Annual General Meeting on 27 April 1979 planning solid achievements in what he described as the Society's 'second era.' Committee members were given specific roles for which they would be the lead person, calling on other members for help. It was not until the Annual General Meeting the following year that the decision to wind up the Society and transfer its assets to Huddersfield Canal Society Ltd could be made. The Committee members then became Directors of the Company, although collectively they were known as the Council of Management rather than the more formal Board of Directors. The new company was registered on 28 May 1980 and soon afterwards as a Charity.

Chris Farrar appreciated that no progress could be made by fighting BW. HCS had gained the respect of Area Engineer John Freeman and Principal Engineer North David Pyrah, but agreement for work by volunteers was still hamstrung because BW could not legally take on the extra maintenance costs on a remainder waterway. A solution was finally found following a chance meeting on the train to London between Chris Farrar and David Pyrah. BW would allow HCS to carry out exploratory work removing concrete cascades and rubble infill from lock chambers, while the Society investigated the possibility of local authorities making annual payments to cover the extra costs. If that support was forthcoming BW would then allow full restoration.

To demonstrate the benefits of restoration and achieve maximum publicity, three projects were concentrated on. The canal towpath through Uppermill was already a popular walk for local people and visitors. If the canal was dredged from the Museum Basin here, Dungebooth and Lime Kiln Locks were restored and a short length of new canal built to link to Wool Road, Dobcross, a trip boat could demonstrate the popularity of a restored canal. Secondly, although it might not be possible to run trips into Standedge Tunnel, the repair and use by the Society of the former tunnel-keepers' cottages at Tunnel End seemed achievable. The idyllic location would be attractive to visitors. Finally, as the only connection to the national network that might be possible in the short-term, the Society proposed the restoration of the canal between Ashton-under-Lyne and Stalybridge.

Local consultations in Uppermill had been started by Peter Freeman and the Saddleworth Historical Society was keen to jointly promote the project. The Society joined with HCS in publishing a report *The Canal in Uppermill: Action for Restoration*. Spelling out the benefits for Uppermill – the canal would link the Museum, the Tame Valley Warden Centre at Brownhill (by Lime Kiln Lock) and Wool Road where the Historical Society was repairing the roof of a small canalside warehouse – it also pointed out that if the problems of restoration could be resolved here there was 'no good reason to doubt that the entire canal could be restored.' Copies were sent to BW, Oldham and Greater Manchester Councils, Saddleworth Parish Council, MPs and councillors. John Maynard explained the scheme to a meeting of the Parish Council. By the middle of 1980 BW had given their blessing. The Parish Council, the District Council and the Tame Valley Joint Committee, composed of county councillors and councillors from the Districts of Oldham, Tameside and Stockport, had approved the scheme. Society Vice Chairman David Sumner took the lead as project officer. He was working for

The tunnel-keepers' cottages at Tunnel End, Marsden, and the portal to Standedge Tunnel. *(HCS)*

Unicon Holdings, a group of companies chaired by Hugh Wainwright, who would be vital to the Society. David persuaded local authority officers that he should attend their working party meetings before the Tame Valley Joint Committee, and that they should investigate making annual payments to cover the additional cost of maintenance. A planning application was submitted by Bob Dewey for the new concrete channel to be built at the foot of the embankment where Wool Road had been widened blocking the canal. An appeal for funds was made and it was announced in *Pennine Link* that work would start the following year.

Council member Trevor Ellis was given responsibility for developing Tunnel End Cottages. The two cottages were boarded up and semi-derelict. As a visitor centre they would show the importance of this secluded spot where encircling hills emphasised the dramatic mouth of Standedge Tunnel. BW was willing to lease the cottages and the West Yorkshire County Council was interested in one as a base for the Countryside Ranger Service. Small working parties were held through the winter of 1980–81 to clear rubbish and make the cottages watertight, but major repairs were needed.

Earlier in 1980 Chris Farrar and other members inspected a trip boat that the Grantham Canal Restoration Society had for sale. Only 14ft (4.2m) long by 5ft (1.5m) beam, this small twelve-seater could be towed on a trailer between different parts of the canal, the shallow draft was essential on a silted canal and it looked as near to 'a proper canal boat' as any tiny version was likely to look. An offer was accepted and the boat was brought to Slaithwaite where a local doctor allowed it to be stored and worked on in his basement. The engine was beyond repair and John Maynard, a professional electrical engineer, designed a new electrical power system created from the controls and motors of an old fork lift truck. Chloride Batteries loaned batteries free of charge. The engine was scrapped, the boat repainted and, signwritten by HCS member Ron Buckley, renamed *Stan* (short for Standedge!). Time was also desperately short to have *Stan* ready for the Tameside Festival in July – so short that, when *Stan* was carried through the streets in the parade on its trailer for Slaithwaite Carnival, John and his helpers continued frantically wiring out of sight, but *Stan* could not run at the Festival. The distance that could be run was not known and the embarrassment of running out of battery power seemed inevitable.

The 1979 Tameside Canals Festival chaired by David Sumner had been a huge success with around 20,000 people attending throughout the weekend of 4 and 5 August, and the Festival in 1980 was equally successful at spreading the word. The message-delivering canoe party now extended to ten canoes and two scout troops. David Sumner listed seventeen helpers in *Pennine Link* but they were only the ones with a named role – publicity officer, moorings officer, trade stands officer, entertainments officer, rota officer etc. It was a mammoth task involving many members to mount these events.

In September 1980 Richard Wainwright, MP for Colne Valley, officially named *Stan* as part of the Society's contribution to Marsden Festival, caught by television cameras and attracted by the idea of boat trips on the derelict canal. Trips were run every weekend through the autumn in Uppermill to publicise the proposed restoration work. Saddleworth Historical Society allowed the batteries to be charged at the museum and the crews learned a zigzag route to avoid overhanging branches and underwater obstacles. Despite occasional worries about the electrics, *Stan* continued to perform in 1981 taking full loads of passengers to see the restoration work beginning at Dungebooth Lock.

On Saturday 4 April 1981, after a trip on *Stan* from the Museum Basin, writer and television personality Anthony Burton ceremonially began breaking-up the concrete capping of Dungebooth Lock. 4 April was chosen as the date when in 1794 the Act of Parliament was passed and in 1811 the whole canal was open to navigation. Two locks needed restoring with new gates and a short infilled section required rebuilding, and it needed to be done quickly to be credible in this popular location. Waterway Recovery Group turned up in force, and by the official opening one third of the concrete capping had been removed from the lock. A three-day working party was arranged with visiting volunteers from Waterway Recovery Group over the Spring Bank Holiday, and work continued most weekends throughout the year with Graham Maskell taking over as project manager. Small financial donations were received, £500 from the Oldham Lottery and £1,100 from the Shell Oil Co.'s awards scheme, and many new members were recruited from onlookers at the lockside.

Narrow boat *Stan* at Uppermill, autumn 1980. *(David Finnis)*

Above: Writer and broadcaster Anthony Burton starts the excavation of Dungebooth Lock, Uppermill,
4 April 1981. The onlookers include Huddersfield Canal Society Chairman, Chris Farrar, the Mayor of Oldham, Councillor John Crowther and David Chadderton from Saddleworth Historical Society (thirrd, fourth and fifth from left). *(David Finnis)*

Left: Graham Maskell attacks the reinforced concrete capping at Dungebooth Lock, Uppermill. *(Bob Dewey)*

The planning application for the rebuilding of the infilled section at Wool Road was delayed when Oldham Council asking for more detailed drawings. These were paid for by Unicon Holdings as a free gift to the Society. Before the application was decided Saddleworth Parish Council arranged a public meeting to discuss the whole issue of restoration. Anglers complained that they had lost fish stocks – although volunteer workers claimed to have seen no dead fish. The meeting on 20 July 1981 in the Civic Hall in Uppermill was packed. Representatives of Slaithwaite Anglers warned that, although the canal may be ideal for fishing now, left to its own devices it would silt up like lengths in the Colne Valley that were too shallow to support fish. The Countryside Warden Service thought that the canal should be enjoyed by the whole community. The Parish Council recommended that Oldham Council grant planning permission. And that duly happened.

Stan continued giving trips to and from Dungebooth Lock until it was moved to Ashton for the Tameside Canals Festival in July. Chaired this time by Colin Chadwick, the weather again smiled and over £2,000 was raised. Shortly before the Festival Chris Farrar stood down as Chairman. He had a new job in Surrey. He had fulfilled his promise of a new era for the Society with work at last work taking place on the canal. Progress was being made on other fronts too as Vice Chairman David Sumner took over as Chairman. West Yorkshire County Council had offered £5,000 towards re-roofing the cottages at Tunnel End, and it was agreed that HCS would sub-let one cottage to the County for the Countryside Ranger Service. The Estates Department at BW was so slow producing the promised lease that the County Council took over negotiations on the basis that they would then sub-let to the Society. Even then the lease was not signed until well into 1982. The third project – to restore the canal between Ashton-under-Lyne and Stalybridge – had a bumpier ride. It had often been on the agenda at the Tame Valley Joint Committee. Greater Manchester Council (GMC) considered taking on the project using government grants. Nothing came of that, but it was thought that, however the scheme continued, GMC would grasp the maintenance issue. The best way forward might be to kick-start the project with a 'Big Dig' involving hundreds of volunteers. Waterway Recovery Group agreed to plan for that and to help HCS volunteers who would move here after the Uppermill locks were finished.

The *Huddersfield Canals Towpath Guide* was launched in a blaze of publicity at the Colne Valley Museum, Golcar on 22 August 1981. A beautifully produced and illustrated eighty-page book, this was published by HCS with the help of loans from West Yorkshire County Council. Edited by *Pennine Link* editor Diane Charlesworth, it contained sections on the history of the Huddersfield Broad and Narrow Canals, wildlife found along the canals, angling, details of the engineering works and a pub guide. The main part was a description of walking the towpath from the junction with the Calder & Hebble Navigation at Cooper Bridge to the junction with the Ashton Canal at Whitelands Road, Ashton-under-Lyne. David Finnis maximised the publicity from this and many other events organised to spread the word and raise money. Hardly a week went by when HCS did not feature in local newspapers or on local radio or television. A large iced cake in the shape of a narrow boat was the prize in a 'Guess the Weight' competition at one of the Tameside Canals Festivals. HCS regularly took part in the Mayor's Parade in Huddersfield, Slaithwaite Carnival and similar events. Floats were decorated with amazing ingenuity in the shape of narrow boats or *Stan* was taken on a trailer, accompanied by balloons, streamers, 'Restore Huddersfield Canal' stickers to hand out and very loud music. Towpath walks were held, and sponsored pub crawls. *Pennine Link* was improving too, now being Xerox copied.

Two events brought national publicity. HCS had attended most of the IWA National Rallies with a caravan or tent, an exhibition and sales material, but the 1981 rally was on the doorstep. Many members descended on the site at Dock Street, Leeds, to blitz the festival and visitors with 'Restore Huddersfield Canal' stickers. A policeman even proudly wore one over his helmet badge! And the message was spread widely by the Mikron Theatre Company's production of *Where's our Cut?* which introduced the Diggles to a national audience in 1979

Left: David Finnis hands a publicity leaflet to Eric Crosland alongside the Slaithwaite Carnival float. Brian Badminton prepares to address the crowds with the microphone under the watchful eye of the 'Diggles' at the tunnel mouth. *(HCS)*

Below: The 1980 Mikron Theatre Company production of *Where's Our Cut?* Cast: Mark Strickson, Mike Lucas, Sarah Wilson and Julie Brennon. *(Mikron Theatre Company)*

and 1980. Named after Artistic Director Mike Lucas and his friend Ron Legge, the Mikron Theatre Company have toured the waterways nationally every summer since 1972 on *Tyseley*, a converted working boat, putting on shows in village halls and pubs, making their unique brand of high quality theatre accessible to a wide audience. In *Where's our Cut?* Napoleon, Rita, Boadicea and Stanley Diggle (performed initially by Mike Lucas, Sandra Moore, Carol Prior and Chris Whittingham) told the story of the Huddersfield Narrow Canal with music, songs and humour. Mr Brown and Mr Outram discussed the problems of building a tunnel with insufficient money, Stanley and Napoleon Diggle sang while 'legging' through the tunnel and the show ended with the very apt title song *Where's our Cut?*

8 Jobs for the Boys, Girls and Me

In February 1982 David Sumner asked me to join the HCS Council to develop new projects on the canal. My first wife Sue had been typing *Pennine Link* for some time, and we had attended working parties at Uppermill – although I was better at talking about restoration than wielding a shovel. Sue graduated to editing *Pennine Link*. Under her control it became a professionally printed magazine and she won the first of many IWA awards for the best canal society magazine. At Uppermill volunteers worked every weekend with help from visiting groups. Dungebooth Lock was cleared of rubble infill on Sunday 4 July 1982. Hugh Wainwright watched it being measured for lockgates that his company had agreed to donate. In August, a two-week Waterway Recovery Group work camp was held that cleared the chamber of Lime Kiln Lock. Crompton Traction Batteries donated a second set of batteries so that *Stan* could run more trips and West Yorkshire County Council was repairing the roof and floors of the cottages at Tunnel End.

David Sumner and Bob Dewey met County Councillor Peter Scott, the chairman of planning at GMC, showing him slides of the canal. They reported on progress at Uppermill to a meeting of the Tame Valley Joint Committee and stressed the need for financial support to top up BW's maintenance budget. BW had only sanctioned exploratory work and would not allow completion of the locks without financial assistance. The GMC Recreation and Arts Committee agreed to make small annual payments when the scheme was complete. This recognition by one of the local authorities that they had a role in the restoration of the canal was a massive step forward, and BW soon approved the restoration work.

HCS membership was rising rapidly – but so were expectations. There would have to be a volunteer project to follow the Uppermill locks, and we had to find the money to rebuild the infilled section beyond at Wool Road, but restoration of the entire canal was beyond the scope of volunteers or the Society's ability to fund-raise. Nationally, the country was in a bad way. Thirty years of government manipulation of the economy to keep full employment and maintain Britain's status as a world power had ended in 1976 when the government of Jim Callaghan was forced to borrow from the International Monetary Fund. The year before, inflation had reached 35%. The trade unions had fought spending cuts and wage restraint leading, directly, to industrial chaos and public sector strikes, and, indirectly, to Mrs Thatcher's government being elected in 1979 and intent on curbing union power and putting the finances of the country in a better shape by controlling the money supply. The medicine was necessary but the side effects were dramatic. By 1983 inflation fell to 5% but thousands of jobs were being lost. Over three million people would eventually be unemployed. The old industries, including the textile mills of the Colne and Tame Valleys, were effectively shut down – or reduced to little more than a few token businesses. Even the extreme right of an increasingly right-wing Conservative Party saw that something must be done. Money was made available through the Manpower Services Commission (MSC) to create temporary jobs and provide new skills to get people back to work. Job creation schemes had started in a small way in the 1970s. The Surrey and Hampshire Canal Society restored the fourteen Deepcut Locks on the Basingstoke Canal between 1977 and 1983 with MSC workers. A joint West Yorkshire County Council and Calderdale Council scheme had now started on the Rochdale Canal – the lockgates for Dungebooth and Lime Kiln locks would come from that scheme's

Waterway Recovery Group volunteers at Lime Kiln Lock, August 1982. *(Trevor Ellis)*

Opposite: David Finnis and County Councillor John Sully preparing to cycle down the east side of the canal at Tunnel End, Marsden. *(HCS)*

workshop. BW had been reluctant to allow MSC schemes, unlike the local authority-owned Basingstoke or company-owned Rochdale Canals, fearing the unions would bring the workforce out on strike to protect 'real jobs'. By the early 1980s, as unemployment grew, that concern diminished and small MSC projects were beginning on other BW canals.

HCS had campaigned for restoration because of the canal's historic importance, as a link between the Midlands and Yorkshire waterways, and because of the environmental benefits. We changed tack. With traditional industries in almost terminal decline, new jobs resulting from a restored canal must be a benefit for all the community. I wrote a report published in November 1982, dryly entitled *A Report on the Job Creation Potential of the Huddersfield Narrow Canal as a Navigable Waterway*, estimating the number of jobs that would be created if the canal was restored. If jobs were created at the same rate as on canals for which published research was available in businesses such as boat hire, boatyards, trip boats, restaurant and hotel boats; in cafés, shops and pubs; in extra maintenance staff; and from additional trade from day trippers, together with extra trade at suppliers to these businesses, there would be around 310 extra jobs.

If West Yorkshire and Kirklees Councils were to emulate the Rochdale Canal scheme in the Colne Valley something big was needed to dent the unemployment figures. The obvious area to tackle was between Marsden and Slaithwaite. With a lot of help from Trevor Ellis, David Finnis, Bob Dewey and Eric Crosland, I noted the work required, produced maps and wrote a report. David Finnis brought in other community groups, we agreed the draft of the report with them and Sue McBride arranged the graphic design, layout and printing. At the end of 1982 HCS published *A Proposal for the Restoration of the Huddersfield Narrow Canal from Marsden to Slaithwaite* as a glossy illustrated document in association with the Colne Valley Society, Marsden Community Association, Slaithwaite and District Angling Club and Pennine Heritage. The canal passed through attractive Pennine countryside rising by a series of locks from the centre of Slaithwaite to Marsden and Tunnel End. Restored it would be a linear park in an area where the local authorities hoped to attract recreational and tourist development. Work could be by one of the new Community Programme schemes being promoted by the MSC to create temporary jobs in areas of high unemployment. Copies were sent to council officers, to the Tourist Board, and to councillors, MPs and MEPs.

Before we had any response we looked again at the canal between Ashton and Stalybridge. After its end-on junction with the Ashton Canal at Whitelands Road bridge, the canal passed through three locks which had been variously weired, capped and filled until it reached the culverted bridge at Bayley Street in Stalybridge. A programme of work based on a 'Big Dig' approach had been accepted by the Tame Valley Joint Committee. After the 'Big Dig' environmental works and dredging would be carried out by GMC while volunteers would complete the locks. GMC anticipated meeting the additional maintenance costs. Then Alan Jervis, the Chairman of Waterway Recovery Group, reported in October 1982 that a 'Big Dig' was impractical. The arrangements for draining the canal were limited and the canal so silted that it could take weeks to drain sufficiently for hundreds of volunteers to work. And the Ashton and Peak Forest Canals would be deprived of water from the Huddersfield Narrow closing the Cheshire Ring. The intention to re-open this length of canal had been declared, however. We decided to suggest another MSC scheme. Together with Alan Jervis, I wrote a report stressing the benefits and describing the scheme. Alan produced a specification of work. Like the Marsden/Slaithwaite report it was a very professional looking publication with a superb cover designed by Sue McBride. Again copies were sent to the local authorities, councillors and MPs.

We had taken a considerable risk printing glossy reports. It was asking a lot to expect local authorities to spend on the canal when they were starved of funds by a government set on cutting public spending. There would be a significant capital cost to top up the money from the MSC to pay for lockgates and materials, and a revenue cost for annual maintenance payments. But there were environmental and social benefits and GMC had already agreed to underwrite the maintenance costs of the canal in Uppermill. Years of lobbying and contact with councillors and council officers began to pay off. HCS had gained respect and credibility, and the glossy reports were backed up by the dry professional report on jobs. IWA's *Waterways* magazine commented that this 'hard-hitting report [was] just the thing to make local

Fitting the lockgates, Dungebooth Lock, Uppermill, July 1983. The photographer on the bank is Ann Crosland. Trevor Ellis is in the lock chamber. David Sumner (extreme right) displays remarkably clean overalls. *(Bob Dewey)*

authorities sit up and take notice.' John Sully, the chairman of West Yorkshire Recreation and Arts Committee, was introduced to the canal by David Sumner and David Finnis and interviewed at Tunnel End by Yorkshire Television. He was so impressed that he arranged a trip to show Kirklees councillors the Rochdale scheme and he even contributed an article to *Pennine Link*. George Speight, the chairman of planning at Kirklees, saw the Marsden/Slaithwaite project as just what was needed in the upper Colne Valley.

Almost the whole of 1983 passed in meetings with local authority officers, with the MSC and with BW, where we first met Alex Thomson BW's manager for special employment schemes. Real progress was made with Marsden/Slaithwaite, but Ashton/Stalybridge stalled because GMC thought it could be eligible for government grants and MSC work in Tameside would be better east of Stalybridge. Kirklees planners John Miller and David Wyles, and Dan Hogan and Geoff Clegg in the Recreation and Arts Department at West Yorkshire, sought advice from Dick Booth, the manager of the Rochdale scheme, and from BW. We provided costs for volunteer work and Society members Eric Crosland, David Irvine and Ian Mitchell even produced a list of tools required in a lockgate workshop.

Both lock chambers in Uppermill were ready for lockgates in the summer of 1983. Unloaded from a truck in Uppermill, the gates were floated up the canal tied to empty oil drums for buoyancy. A scaffolding gantry was erected over the locks to fit the gates and, just before the Tameside Festival, Dungebooth Lock had gates generously provided by Hugh Wainwright and his company Unicon Holdings. The gates for Lime Kiln were fitted after the Festival on 11 and 12 August.

On Saturday 10 September 1983 Tunnel End Cottages were opened by County Councillor Sykes, the Chairman of West Yorkshire County Council, as the centrepiece of a Festival arranged on the site. A large contingent of councillors, BW representatives and other VIPs attended. The exhibition in the Society's cottage told the story of canals with superb artwork by Sue McBride and borrowed canalware and artefacts. A counter providing information and souvenirs was staffed by volunteers on weekends and bank holidays at first, but soon the local authority provided staff so the centre could open full-time. The second cottage had a countryside display provided by the county council and would be a base for the Countryside Ranger Service.

An essential part of the plan for Uppermill was to show the re-opened canal to the public. *Stan* was too small for a regular trip boat. Hugh Wainwright came up trumps again, buying a 70ft (21m) narrow boat from the Coombe Hill Canal Trust. This had a double-ended iron hull made up from the front parts of two old working boats, fitted with an open-sided steel roof and seats for forty-eight passengers. It was powered by a BMC diesel engine that drove an unusual water jet unit that could be turned to steer the boat and propel it in either direction. This double-ended nature was needed at Uppermill where, until the infilled section below Wool Road was rebuilt, the boat could only be turned at the Museum Basin. The boat was repaired and repainted by Unicon Marine and leased to HCS. We named it *Benjamin Outram*. A massive crane lifted *Benjamin Outram* – soon shortened to *Benjie* – over the canalside trees into the Museum Basin at Uppermill on a gloriously sunny day in April 1984. John Maynard, Vince Willey and other experienced crews gave training sessions and public trips began on the Good Friday. The canal had not been dredged. There was no access for land-based plant and we could not afford to hire and crane in a dredger. But volunteers in waders had removed large items of debris, raking aside the obvious high spots, and *Benjie* successfully gave trips over the Easter Holiday period although with frequent stops to sort out mechanical problems.

The engine was given an overhaul before the official lock opening by Councillor J.K. Leyden the Mayor on Saturday 26 May 1984, but the jet steering remained troublesome. *Benjamin Outram* was scrubbed and polished but, as the VIP trip to the locks started from the Museum Basin, the steering jammed. Contingency plans had been made and Sonny, the Ashton Packet Boat Co.'s horse, was standing by to tow the boat – much to the delight of the guests. Uppermill Junior Brass Band played as the ribbon was cut by the mayor and mayoress. A buffet was laid on at the Brownhill Visitor Centre alongside the canal just beyond Lime Kiln Lock and, after the speeches a vintage bus took the guests to the Lock Opening Festival at the

Benjamin Outram is launched over the trees in Uppermill, April 1984. *(David Finnis)*

Councillor Leyden, the Mayor of Oldham, cuts the tape to re-open Dungebooth Lock, 26 May 1984. *(HCS)*

playing fields in Uppermill. Uppermill Brass Band played and Saddleworth Morris Men danced. There were craft stalls, kiddies rides, a bouncing castle, side-shows, boatmen's games and the inevitable beer tent. As part of his speech David Sumner announced that HCS had been named by Councillor Stanley Dawson as one of the charities to benefit from his Mayor's Appeal in Kirklees that year.

The jet unit remained troublesome but volunteer boat crews operated every weekend for the rest of the year. It was difficult to find crews to meet the demand for weekday trips, so in 1985 HCS franchised the operation to Society member Harold Nield who lived by the canal in Uppermill. Apart from relieving the problem of finding enough volunteers, many of whom continued to work for Harold, this showed that private sector investment would flow from a restored canal.

Meanwhile on 9 December 1983 Kirklees Council's Development & Technical Services Committee had considered the Marsden/Slaithwaite project. On 9 January 1984 a similar item was considered by West Yorkshire County Council's Recreation & Arts Committee. Both committees agreed. About fifty people would be employed to restore nearly three miles of canal and nineteen locks. A West Yorkshire engineer, Ian Preston, was appointed to manage the project. Kirklees was negotiating the lease of premises for a lockgate workshop. This was a major triumph and, even more than GMC's financial commitment to maintenance, the beginning of a long lasting partnership between HCS and the local authorities.

GMC and Tameside had not forgotten about the Ashton/Stalybridge scheme. The Tame Valley Joint Committee agreed with GMC that an MSC scheme should begin east of Stalybridge, but, unlike Kirklees, Tameside preferred to act as agents providing administrative support to independently managed projects rather than manage projects themselves. I had also been talking to John Billington, a planner with Oldham Council, about the possibility of a scheme in the Greenfield to Diggle area but the council preferred schemes in less favoured parts of the district. We wondered whether HCS might have to manage an MSC scheme itself in Oldham and Tameside. Then John Hey, Tameside Council's MSC co-ordinator, approached us. Like Kirklees, Tameside wanted large projects employing big numbers. Meeting David

Sumner in August 1983, John asked whether HCS would join with others to manage a Community Programme scheme on the canals in Tameside – the Ashton and Peak Forest as well as the Huddersfield Narrow. The opportunity was too good to miss, so the Tameside Canals Development Association was formed as an informal group consisting of David Sumner and myself, representing HCS, David Brown of the Peak Forest Canal Society and Guy Martin from the Manchester Branch of IWA with Frank Ruffley as chairman. Frank came with the Tameside connection. He was a Labour councillor and chairman of the Social Services Committee. He knew the political system. He knew Ashton and Stalybridge. And he knew canals, often being seen at Portland Basin. His patience would prove invaluable and, being retired, he was willing to devote time to the Association.

With Tameside Council agreeing to act as managing agents, a scheme was put to the MSC proposing towpath repair and environmental improvement on the Peak Forest Canal, but making clear that the Association intended to move on to restoration of the Huddersfield Narrow. I wrote yet another report *The Huddersfield Narrow Canal: No longer a derelict eyesore through Tameside*. The details of the work required to restore the canal from Stalybridge to the district boundary between Mossley and Greenfield had been prepared by Peter Freeman and a group of Society members. The MSC approved the scheme and interviews were held for the manager. A quantity surveyor, Stephen Whitby (generally known as Steve) was appointed. He started work and began recruiting staff on 1 May 1984. The first year would cost £320,000 with the wages and salaries coming from the MSC. Alex Thomson agreed that BW would provide £4,000. The Tame Valley Warden Service gave £1,000. A further £1,000 was donated by BW to buy a reconditioned engine for a 46ft (14m) working narrow boat that was acquired and named *Ruffley's Little Tinker* together with two working pontoons, a mini tractor, and a roller for the towpath. Work began with seventy-seven employees behind the Cheshire Ring public house in Hyde to the south of Ashton where Steve established a base in two portacabins.

Meanwhile on 8 May work began on the Marsden/Slaithwaite project, with thirty labourers, five supervisors and two craftsmen. A workshop at Spring Grove Mills, Linthwaite was prepared and wood ordered for the first set of lockgates. An access was constructed and fenced to an old BW-owned dredgings tip off Warehouse Hill, Marsden, where it was again intended to tip dredgings and set up site cabins. Work began in Marsden on the capped Lock 39E above Warehouse Hill bridge. Regular progress meetings were held chaired by Alex

Ruffley's Little Tinker – the Society's first work boat. *(HCS)*

Work beginning on the Kirklees Council/West Yorkshire County Council job creation scheme at Marsden.
(Keith Gibson)

Thomson that I attended on behalf of HCS. A site inspection at the first meeting after work started showed an excavator working on Lock 40E and a gang clearing the by-wash to Lock 38E. In September Ian Preston, the manager, reported in *Pennine Link* that already more than 4,000 tons of spoil had been removed, four pounds were dredged and four lock chambers were ready for gates. Before the end of the year gates would be fitted to Locks 39E and 42E. Although dredging would be by land-based machine wherever possible, a BW dredger, *Fox*, and mud hoppers arrived in November by which time forty-eight people were employed.

HCS was spending serious amounts of money; the lockgates at Lime Kiln and the working party had not come cheap, nor had the exhibition at Tunnel End. The commitment to the Tameside Canals Development Association might be costly when the scheme transferred to restoration work. The festivals continued at Portland Basin, chaired in 1982 and 1984 by Laurence Sullivan. The 1982 festival continued the success of previous years with massive numbers of visitors, a lot of publicity and raising money, but it rained in 1984. It poured all weekend in 1983 when Vince Willey and his helpers sloshed around in the mud, but still made money as well as gaining publicity. There were more pleasant ways of raising money. David Finnis organised a sponsored pub crawl with walkers dressed in Diggle costumes – apart from Bob Dewey who for some obscure reason had a mammoth costume! The Diggles and the mammoth were in *The Huddersfield Examiner* and interviewed by Radio Leeds. The smaller Diggles were so popular that sewing evenings were needed to keep up with demand. Raffles were held and a sponsored walk, Toepath '82, raised nearly £3,000 from over 200 walkers, an effort beaten the following year when Toepath '83 attracted over 300 walkers and raised almost £4,000. A Cheese and Wine & Mikron evening at the Brownhill Visitor Centre raised funds from a performance of *Where's our Cut?* and a flag day was held in Huddersfield town centre in December 1983. It was very cold. A craft fair at Tunnel End the weekend after was warmer. A tenth birthday party was held for Society members at *The Diggle Hotel* on 19 April 1984, and – considerably more sober – a coffee morning in Huddersfield Town Hall organised by Ann Crosland.

The cascaded Lock 31W before the start of work. *(Keith Gibson)*

Everyone but a complete recluse in the Tame & Colne Valleys had heard of HCS. The Society had almost 1,000 members and, despite spending heavily, nearly £15,000 in the bank. Whether publicity would continue at the same level was doubtful, however, as David Finnis resigned. He had a new job and his employers were not keen on the press confusing whether he was publicising them or the canal.

It was difficult to find a scheme for volunteers after Uppermill because the local authorities would not make maintenance payments for more lengths of canal unless restoration created jobs with an MSC scheme. Then we found that locks 31W and 32W at Diggle had been bought by Oldham Council when land alongside was landscaped in the 1970s. The council agreed that they would allow volunteer working parties without worrying about future maintenance provided BW accepted the plan of work. I hoped that they would. I had a dumper in my garage. In the meantime Graham Maskell arranged working party visits to other canals but, after his mammoth stint as organiser at Uppermill, he felt unable to devote his spare time to another project. Society Vice Chairman Trevor Ellis took on the task. He agreed with BW on how the volunteers would go about restoring the locks – which was a much larger job than at Uppermill as the lock chambers were substantially demolished.

Planning permission for the Wool Road infilled section had been granted in 1982, but we had no success in finding grants to build the new channel. I was talking to GMC planners Steve Ankers and Peter Davey about this and other projects. They were finding grants hard to come by for the Ashton/Stalybridge section. David Sumner was talking to their colleague Peter Webster and their boss Robert Maund and to Peter Scott, the Chairman of Planning. David wrote to County Councillor Scott setting out the benefits of full restoration of the canal. Whether as a result of that letter, or entirely coincidentally, on 11 July 1984 the GMC Planning Committee decided that the council would seek to re-open both the Huddersfield Narrow and the Rochdale Canals in the county over a ten to fifteen year period. That should have been wonderful news, but the Metropolitan County Councils' future was uncertain.

Without realistic costs we could take the Wool Road infilled section no further, so we sought prices from contractors. Quotations were received and in October 1984 I wrote to GMC asking for financial help. Very soon I had a reply which said 'the Society may struggle to secure sufficient grant-aid for this work … and I would appreciate your confirmation that you are happy for GMC to proceed with the implementation of [the] scheme.' I telephoned Steve Ankers at GMC. Did he really mean that the County Council would take on the scheme? Yes, and he would recommend that to the committee. Very gratefully we immediately confirmed that we had no objections to GMC taking over the scheme. The Council's Planning Committee decided in August 1985 to proceed with the work – an absolutely crucial decision as councils on both sides of the Pennines would now be actively involved in restoration.

There had been more good news a few months earlier too when the same committee agreed to make a grant of £10,000 for the volunteer work at Diggle.

Sadly the granting of funds for restoration of the canal by GMC and their decision to adopt a policy of restoring the canal came too late in the life of the council. The Thatcher government's wish to limit public spending had, it was said, been thwarted by profligate local authorities. Mrs Thatcher was convinced that something must be done to clip the wings of local government. The Metropolitan County Councils and the Greater London Council were to be disbanded as a warning to the others. The canal restoration movement had benefited from the ability of the county authorities to put capital into local projects from the proceeds of a minute proportion of their income. After 1986 canal restoration would be more expensive for district councils who would not be able to draw on funds from around the region.

9 A Millionaire Society

The impending disbandment of the County Councils was a setback but it strengthened Chairman David Sumner's resolve that HCS must have a clear strategy, knowing what we wanted to achieve next. We had been talking to Jim Saunders of engineering consultants W.S. Atkins & Partners. He was convinced that the benefits of complete restoration of the canal would have a far higher value than the cost of carrying out the work. We would need to set on consultants to prove this before we could successfully apply for grants for work beyond the scope of volunteers or MSC workers.

Stewart Sim, who had taken over as Area Engineer at BW, agreed that a meeting of the local authorities was the way ahead. It would be the first occasion when councillors from all five local authorities had met to discuss the canal and could be the defining moment in the political campaign to restore the canal. So on 18 October 1984 the Society and W.S. Atkins & Partners held a presentation to members and officers of the councils. Our guests were taken through the restored Uppermill locks on *Benjamin Outram*. A coach visit to see the work of Ian Preston's team at Marsden was followed by lunch at the Coach & Horses pub on Standedge. David Sumner spoke with great authority on the need for a joint approach to restoration of the canal for the benefit of the valley communities. Jim Saunders addressed the issue of a Cost Benefit Study, which he recommended as a key step. County Councillors Sully and Pratt from West Yorkshire thought the study could be counterproductive as it would show a very high cost, and members of the district councils were worried that the cost of work particularly in Stalybridge could be way beyond what could be met, but all agreed that the time was right for a joint committee, and they would recommend that their councils take part.

There was no time for GMC to proceed with the Ashton/Stalybridge project which left the way open for the Tameside Canals Development Association to take on that scheme before moving east of Stalybridge. Supported by subtle lobbying from HCS, Frank Ruffley wrote to Tameside, GMC & BW requesting permission to do the work, asking for financial aid towards materials and plant and asking that GMC enter into a maintenance agreement to cover the extra costs. The MSC was offering well over 100 employees for the second year. The association could not continue as a loose association with no legal status. It was a big step to take on the responsibility for so many employees, but the best way forward was for HCS, with its status as a limited company and a charity, to set up a subsidiary company to take over the scheme. There were community benefits in retaining the local name, so the new subsidiary company was formed as Tameside Canals Ltd. Frank Ruffley agreed to stay on as chairman.

BW would provide £10,000 towards the costs. GMC agreed to make a £45,000 grant and to enter into a maintenance agreement with BW. Tameside would provide plant and materials for the continuing Peak Forest towpath works. A new site for the portacabin offices was found on land owned by the Senior Service cigarette factory alongside lock 2W. The land was rent-free and the company put in an electricity supply to the offices. Steve Whitby bought our first new vehicle, a Bedford Astra van. Work continued on the Peak Forest towpath and on environmental projects but there were engineering problems before work could start on the Huddersfield Narrow – the water level sewer pipe below Lock 1W, and the lock tail bridge at Lock 2W had been widened to improve access to the Senior Service factory. It would obstruct the tailgates of the lock. The bridge could be altered so that lockgates could be fitted, but neither here nor at Lock 1W, where Whitelands Road bridge had also been altered, was there space for lockgates to be opened and closed by pushing on traditional balance beams. BW agreed that they would arrange the design and manufacture of a hydraulic mechanism to operate the gates.

BW was in what might be termed its hydraulic era. They instructed that paddle gear at the locks should be hydraulically operated. Many enthusiasts viewed the loss of traditional mechanical gear with dismay and believed the hydraulic gear to be inherently dangerous because the water flow could not be stopped quickly. There was criticism of the HCS council for not speaking out against hydraulics, but we were not in a strong position to challenge BW, and there was a feeling that, although we should restore the canal with historically accurate paddle gear, the traditional Huddersfield gear fitted to the tail gates of the locks in Uppermill was positively dangerous. It was heavy to use and was operated from a small wooden platform cantilevered out above the canal with no safety rail to prevent a slip.

The Kirklees/West Yorkshire scheme was making rapid progress. By midsummer 1985 fifteen locks and thirteen pounds had been cleared of spoil. Lock numbers 39E–42E at Marsden were complete. And I was still talking to Oldham Council about a possible third MSC scheme in the Greenfield area. Meanwhile volunteers managed by Trevor Ellis started work on locks 31W and 32W at Diggle. The first task was to clear the lock by-washes and rebuild the weirs to them – not easy as the by-washes were piped as much as 6ft (2m) below ground rather than being open channels alongside the locks. Visiting groups from Waterway Recovery Group and the Kennet & Avon Canal trust helped during 1985, but the scale of work meant that volunteers would be working here much longer than they had in Uppermill.

The county councils were considering how best to ensure projects they had been funding continued. HCS kept in close contact with GMC and we were asked to work out a five-year programme of work. With help from Steve Whitby on the costs, I produced a plan for Tameside Canals and volunteers to restore the straightforward parts of the canal between Stalybridge and Diggle. The shortfall between the cost of the work and the MSC funding would be about £45,000 per year. That seemed acceptable to GMC, and by September 1985 we anticipated that the County Council would find a way to leave around £250,000 to pay for this work.

At the same time in West Yorkshire, a Huddersfield County Councillor, Garth Pratt, and County Councillor John Sully, the Chairman of the Recreation & Arts Committee, were busy on behalf of the canal. The council had already shown enthusiasm for waterways with the Rochdale Canal and the joint Kirklees/West Yorkshire MSC schemes, so it was no surprise when on 18 February 1985 the Recreation and Arts Committee decided to build a new bridge at Wakefield Road in Huddersfield. It was a vital step removing a very significant and symbolic barrier to navigation and it would be the first time that a major road crossing of this scale had been restored to navigation on the waterway network anywhere in the country. The old canal bridge had been replaced by small pipes under Wakefield Road, cutting off the short length of the Huddersfield Broad Canal alongside the Huddersfield Polytechnic and the Huddersfield Narrow Canal beyond from the main canal network at Aspley Basin across the six traffic lanes of the road. This would be the first physical obstruction to be removed by employing contractors.

On Wednesday 3 July, at Huddersfield Town Hall, the first meeting of the Huddersfield Narrow Canal Joint Committee was held, chaired by Sir Leslie Young, Chairman of British Waterways Board. Two members of each council and officers of BW were appointed to the committee. David Sumner and Trevor Ellis represented the Society. They had no vote but were expected to take part in discussion and report to members. The work programme for Tameside Canals was reported. It was announced that the Kirklees/West Yorkshire scheme would not stop at Slaithwaite but would continue beyond the infilled section there with the

Progress on the east side. Fitting
lockgates at Lock 32E. *(HCS)*

intention of carrying out all of the straightforward restoration work down to Huddersfield.
GMC told the committee that they were looking into leaving a funding legacy. Officers were
instructed to investigate the possibility of a charitable trust being responsible for this money.
All in all, an excellent day for the canal.

One of the first decisions of the Joint Committee was to support an engineering study of
the alternative routes through Stalybridge. Largely paid for by GMC, with contributions from
HCS and the IWA, this was carried out by Jim Saunders and his colleagues at W.S. Atkins &
Partners who were commissioned by HCS to carry out the study. They considered six possible
routes through or around the town centre. The original route passing through the heart of the
town would bring new life, trade, jobs and income to the town, but it was obstructed by
important business and industrial premises. Alternatively that route could be followed, but
with about half of it in a tunnel below the major employers of Delta Cables and the Millwood
Rubber Co.; this would still require the demolition of a garage business and at least part of
the squash court of the privately owned Castle Hall Sports Centre. It would be expensive and
not particularly attractive. Two alternative arrangements to create a high level route
overlooking the town on the disused railway built to provide four tracks up the valley would
have provided spectacular views, but the town would be by-passed and gain no benefit. The
river route suggested by the Society, utilising the river to by-pass the town centre, connecting
to the canal above Mottram Road at the eastern end and at the aqueduct over the River Tame
at the western end, was more realistic but it had disadvantages. It would require more locks.
The river was at a low level, and crowded with the backs of buildings. Boats could not moor

Left above: Councillor Stanley and Mrs Dawson present a cheque from the Mayor's Charity to Trevor Ellis. *(HCS). Right:* County Councillor Garth Pratt 'cutting the first sod' of the new Wakefield Road Bridge, Huddersfield. *(HCS). Left:* County Councillors John Sully and Garth Pratt cut the tape to open Wakefield Road Bridge. *(HCS)*

on the river section; it was subject to flash floods typical of upland rivers and boaters may have to leave the river quickly. It would be difficult to prevent polluted river water mixing with relatively clean canal water, and there would be high costs of pumping to prevent water being lost to the river. Finally Atkins looked at a compromise between the original and the river routes. This would need a new bridge at the limit of water at Bayley Street to the west and the rebuilding of the canal on its original line from there to the edge of the town centre at Caroline Street. Here the winding course of the river would be divided from the canal only by a minor road and a small factory building that could be demolished with less serious consequences than the buildings on the original route. A total of seven locks would still be required, five in the river, but a sharp bend in the river would be avoided, it would reduce the length of river involved and the connection at Caroline Street would be much easier than that originally suggested where space was limited.

Although members of the Society generally favoured the original route, too many people worked at the factories on that route. We decided that we would publicly support whichever route the council selected when they had studied the report.

At the end of 1985 John Maynard resigned from HCS Council, leaving only Bob Dewey of the original committee. John wrote in *Pennine Link* that restoration of the canal needed 'the enthusiasm of youth, not the caution of old age.' In truth, other council members were now mainly middle-aged, or very soon would be. John became the first Life Member of the Society, always willing to help and make constructive criticism. Shortly before that, Kirklees Councillor Stanley Dawson had presented a cheque for £2,101 to Vice-Chairman Trevor Ellis at Lock 42E, Marsden, that being the Society's proportion of the money he raised for nominated charities in his mayoral year.

The first sod (actually a piece of hot-rolled asphalt) of the bridge was cut by County Councillor Garth Pratt at Wakefield Road on Monday 7 October. The contract went to Streeters (Northern) Ltd. Not only did the company beat the target time, but predicted horrific traffic snarl-ups on Huddersfield's second busiest feeder road never happened. The new bridge was a box culvert structure of thirty-four pre-cast sections installed in three stages. Two major telephone cable ducts and two large cast-iron high pressure water mains had to be re-laid. There was a large turnout of VIPs to see the first boat through early in 1986. David Finnis's replacement as press officer, *Yorkshire Post* journalist Alec Ramsden, ensured the event made the national papers and television. It was a fitting climax to John Sully's career as a County Councillor and a hugely symbolic event when the 44ft (13.4m) narrow boat *Aylesbury Merganser* owned by County Council footpaths officer Wilf Moss nosed under the new bridge. Garth Pratt, who was steering the boat with help from John Sully, mis-quoted Neil Armstrong to say that it was a short journey underneath a six-lane highway, but a major leap forward in the campaign to restore the canal.

Left: Councillor George Speight and County Councillor John Sully prepare to cut the tape at Lock 42E to mark the completion of the first locks at Marsden shortly before the demise of the West Yorkshire County Council in 1986. *(HCS)*. *Right: Stan* tries out the re-opened Lock 42E. Bob Dewey (steering) with Trevor Ellis (with camera), David Wakefield (with cap) and John Maynard. *(HCS)*

Manchester Road Bridge, Hyde on the Peak Forest Canal. Repairs, painting and relaying stone sett paving carried out by Tameside Canals Ltd.

Meanwhile discussions continued with GMC. The financial legacy was to be extended to allow for at least some of the culverted bridges to be replaced by new bridges, so a much larger sum was being talked of as 1985 drew to a close. The council's legal department advised that it would be illegal to pay the money to a trust controlled by serving local authority members or officers. The charitable trust that the Joint Committee was considering was a non-starter, but there would be no restriction on the payment of money to a wholly independent charitable company if that company was committed by its constitution to use the money for the purpose for which it was to be given. The council's solicitor recommended that as HCS already existed as a charitable company, the council should make the money available to the Society.

So it was decided that a grant would be paid to HCS and it would now be of the staggering total of £1,200,000. Before the money was paid BW had to enter into a legal agreement with HCS to allow work to be carried out on the canal, BW had to agree to keep the restored parts of the canal open for public use and to seek an Act of Parliament to restore the rights of navigation removed by the LMS (Canals) Act in 1944, and HCS had to agree to invitelLocal authority nominees onto its Council of Management. When names were suggested those of us who knew them thought these nominees might turn out to be very useful members.

The Society's company secretary, John Fryer, and treasurer, Les Winnard, toiled with the GMC and BW legal departments to get the agreements in place before the demise of the council. Before BW could enter into these agreements the question of the future maintenance of all of the canal west of the Pennines had to be resolved. BW quickly provided details of likely additional costs, and within little more than a few days members of both councils agreed to enter into Maintenance Agreements for the entire length of canal in their district, no doubt as part of a series of urgent decisions consequent on the loss of the county council. Progress was amazingly rapid for such complex negotiations, with good will and enthusiasm shown by all parties.

In February 1986 soon to be ex-County Councillors Peter Scott and Allen Brett (GMC) and John Sully (West Yorkshire) were co-opted to the Society's Council of Management. As part of a general strengthening of the Society's political and financial ability we also extended the GMC brief to include County Councillor Garth Pratt and Ken Goodwin, the chairman of IWA.

Despite all of this activity there was no certainty that we would receive the GMC grant. Tameside and Oldham Councils jointly agreed to grant £45,000 to the Tameside Canals scheme in 1986-1987 under transitional grant arrangements that were being set up in the county to replace County Council funding in the short term.

By the end of 1985 Tameside Canals was employing 170 people and at last working on the Huddersfield Narrow. Lock 3W was a straightforward job of the type we would face on other locks afterwards; the top parts of the chamber walls were unstable and must be rebuilt. Locks 1W and 2W were more complex. The by-wash (the overflow channel around the lock) at lock 1W was blocked off and a new structure was needed. Immediately after the lock the towpath dived into a narrow tunnel under Whitelands Road bridge; the new by-wash would be a pipe buried parallel to the lock and under the stone pathway of the tunnel to emerge into the canal below the bridge. Work could not start until the water authority had removed the water level sewer directly below the lock. That was slow and complex, involving installing a large siphon under the canal bed. Then at Lock 2W, where the walls of the lock needed significant rebuilding, work could not begin until the bridge to the Senior Service factory had been reduced in width. Again Senior Service was helpful, accepting that the bridge was widened at their own risk, and they set on contractors George Dews to modify the bridge. So for most of 1985 we worked on environmental projects – planting trees, repairing footpaths, repairing walls and fences and repairing the stone setted surface of bridges on the Peak Forest Canal.

More and better accommodation was needed for the number of workers, and a workshop to support the scheme. On 13 March 1986 Steve Whitby took the Directors to see a former builders yard at number 239 Mossley Road, Ashton-under-Lyne. There were two brick buildings: a rather ramshackle two-storey office that Tameside Council's Building Unit MSC scheme would refurbish for the cost of materials only, and a single-storey workshop that included a loft for storage. There was a small yard between the two buildings and a larger paved space behind that the council owned and would rent for £500 a year. Although not alongside the canal, access was good and the site was only a few minutes walk from the town centre. The premises were self-contained and could be locked behind the gates. GMC agreed their £45,000 grant, which had not yet been spent because of the delays on the locks, could

239 Mossley Road, Ashton-under-Lyne. The base for Tameside Canals Ltd – later HCS Restoration Ltd – and the Huddersfield Canal Society's new home. (HCS)

The new canal channel at the former infilled section alongside Wool Road, Dobcross. *(HCS)*

be used to purchase and refurbish the property. Steve Whitby was authorised to negotiate a price with the owners and to appoint architects Lockside Design Partnership (who were based in a converted warehouse alongside the Peak Forest Canal locks in Marple) to specify the repairs needed and design the alterations.

I had almost forgotten GMC's decision to rebuild the infilled section of canal between the Brownhill Visitor Centre and Wool Road Basin with all of this excitement. At the eleventh hour in March 1986 a contract was let with Ruttle Plant Hire Ltd of Chorley to construct the new concrete channel. Work started immediately.

On 26 March, with no ceremony whatsoever, John Fryer received a cheque to the value of £1,200,000 from GMC. When he paid it into the bank they were so astounded that they had to telephone the council to confirm it was real. It had been very much touch-and-go to enter into all the agreements in time, with County Hall staff leaving for new jobs with the district councils. Subject to the continuance of the MSC's Community Programme scheme, this grant and the interest on the invested capital could virtually ensure restoration of most of the canal from Ashton to Diggle, except for Stalybridge town centre. But, the best laid plans....

10 The Professionals

The Wool Road infilled section was soon completed, and Tameside Canals was making progress on locks 1W–3W. The bridge to the Senior Service factory was reduced in width and the sewer below lock 1W removed. The trench for the new piped by-wash through the towpath tunnel here needed careful shuttering but Steve Whitby and Site Manager John McLouglin lacked an engineer's support for complex jobs. Fortuitously BW was restructuring. Some of Principal Engineer (North) David Pyrah's responsibilities devolved to Stewart Sim who was promoted to Regional Manager. Steve made David welcome in our new office at Mossley Road to give hands-on engineering advice. Frank Ruffley was often there too, being so busy with Tameside Canals that he had not stood for re-election to the council.

A major topic of discussion at early meetings of the Joint Committee had been a proposed survey of Standedge Tunnel. Around £100,000 could be found for this by BW, the local authorities, the IWA and HCS, but tender prices obtained by BW from consulting engineers were three times that. The Joint Committee decided to appoint Ove Arup & Partners if grants could be found to make up the shortfall. The need to find grants for the survey brought home that the benefits resulting from restoration had to be identified before significant grants could be obtained. The Joint Committee asked HCS to commission a study. Just before the final demise of GMC, David Sumner and I interviewed potential consultants, supported in a panel by representatives of the local authorities and BW. A partnership between L&R Leisure Consultants and economic consultants PIEDA was appointed at an agreed fee of £35,000. Val Beswick and Peter Middleton of L&R were very thorough. The report was an impressive document. It identified the likely benefits of full restoration as the creation of 230 jobs in leisure and tourism, an additional £2 million of expenditure retained in the local economy annually, and the creation of a high quality 'green' backdrop to attract development and businesses to the canal corridor. I was disappointed that the number of jobs was less than my earlier report suggested, but they had gone about the study using formulae that met the strict criteria of the Treasury. Development opportunities were identified, especially the creation of a visitor centre and trips into the tunnel based on the BW warehouse at Tunnel End, but they did not expand on the number of jobs that these might create or on the value of development and businesses attracted to the new waterside environment. There was insufficient length of restored canal from which to foretell that. L&R recommended that HCS appoint a project officer to take the lead in seeking grants, especially for Standedge Tunnel and the visitor centre at Tunnel End. Volunteers could not do all that was required with more daytime meetings, more telephone calls and more complex issues. We thought a better solution would be to appoint a part-time consultant; ideally one of the senior planning staff who had taken early retirement from the Metropolitan Counties. I knew just the man but I doubted he would work for HCS having been the County Planning Officer in South Yorkshire. Michael Thompson (Mike to his friends) had the ability and experience that we needed and shared my enthusiasm for the built environment. He astounded me by agreeing to meet David Sumner and, even more, by saying, 'When can I start?' After this Mike and Steve Whitby took over a huge part of the daytime tasks that volunteers could no longer do.

With the £1.2 million cheque in the bank we considered the options. Steve Whitby, treasurer Les Winnard and I wrote working papers and projected cash flows. Eventually we agreed a work programme that was approved by the Joint Committee in January 1987 based on spending interest only at first. Keeping back as much of the capital as possible would retain money to pump prime major tasks later.

On 29 January 1987 Tameside Council decided on the shortened version of the river route as the preferred route through Stalybridge. The council wished to press ahead with the first stage of that, the rebuilding of the canal through Bayley Street to Caroline Street – which Tameside planner Steve Hughes dubbed Staley Wharf – as soon as possible. Many members of HCS were disappointed that the council did not choose the original route but that had never been likely with the risk to jobs at the factories on that route.

There were Waterway Recovery Group work camps on the Diggle locks in the summer of 1986, and on the Bank Holiday weekend in May 1987, then the Society's own volunteers had a second full weekend using a hired excavator and two dumpers, allowing a big step forward in clearing the chamber of Lock 32W, clearing Lock 31W and rebuilding the tail of that lock.

Tameside Canals now had 160 workers. The programme of work for 1986-1987 would cost nearly £600,000, including environmental works. BW would provide £10,000 and HCS £45,000 towards plant and materials with the rest from the MSC. By the beginning of 1987 Locks 1W-3W were almost complete. The lock chambers had been rebuilt and lockgates made at BW's Stanley Ferry workshop were fitted. Work had begun between Stalybridge and Scout Tunnel. Lock 11W was ready for gates and work had started on locks 9W and 10W. HCS had become the proud owner of a dredger, *Norwood*, and two mud hoppers that BW sold us to add to the growing fleet of *Stan, Benjie, Ruffley's Little Tinker* and *No.2* (a second twelve-seat trip boat powered by an outboard motor). Only a narrow channel was dredged between Ashton and Stalybridge. It was all that we could afford, and the canal through Tameside was a Site of Special Scientific Interest (SSSI). The Nature Conservancy Council described the canal as the best example of a flowing eutrophic (rich in nutrients) water system in Greater Manchester with diverse and prolific plant communities including an exceptional range of pondweeds. Aquatic fauna included fourteen species of mollusc and fresh-water sponges. As the numbers of employees grew Tameside Canals employed an ecologist to survey the canal and negotiate with the Nature Conservancy Council. Dredging profiles and methods of protecting important habitats were devised by ecologists Angela Ganns, Grant McFarlane and Marko Dukta – each of whom was in post for about six months before finding full-time employment. There were difficulties reconciling natural habitats with waterway restoration in other places, but this canal would silt up without restoration and effectively kill-off the ecological interest. Early in 1988 the Nature Conservancy Council approved our plans. A group of students and British Trust for Conservation volunteers retrieved plants from the canal, to be transplanted in less exposed positions or used in environmental work by Tameside Canals, followed by the dredger *Norwood* to clear the channel. Environmental schemes provided work for many staff including a Landscape Architect, Natasha Newbury, in 1987-1988. The five miles of towpath on the Peak Forest Canal in Tameside was completed. At Portland Basin the area in front of the Heritage Centre was stone paved, the massive waterwheel was restored by specialist contractors, and an Anglers Wharf was built so that disabled people could fish from a wheelchair. The old canal arm at Ashton Wharf was dug out to provide moorings at the junction of the Huddersfield Narrow and Ashton Canals. Rubbish was cleared from sites alongside both the Peak Forest and Huddersfield Narrow Canals, trees were planted and footpaths surfaced, including a major new path and landscaping alongside the canal to the north-east of Stalybridge.

The Kirklees scheme was really steaming down the Colne Valley. By August 1987 lockgates were fitted to all of the locks between lock 25E to the west of Slaithwaite and Marsden. Work had also begun east of Slaithwaite where the canal was dredged down to lock 19E and lock 18E was being rebuilt. By the end of the year work was totally concentrated below Slaithwaite and there was local controversy, and in the correspondence columns of newspapers, about the route through the village. The council held an exhibition there in the public library followed

Right: Waterway Recovery Group summer work camp, Lock 31W, Diggle, 1986. *(Trevor Ellis)*

Below: Tameside Canals Ltd working on the Huddersfield Narrow Canal at last. Rebuilding Lock 2W, August 1986. *(HCS)*

Restored Locks 34E and 35E, Marsden. *(Keith Gibson)*

by a public meeting on 9 July 1987 in the Civic Hall. Three options were described: to reinstate the canal along its original alignment, to use that route but enclosed in a tunnel below the grassed area and car park in the village centre, or to by-pass the centre altogether by canalising the River Colne. Many local residents were anxious to keep the attractive grassed area with its cherry trees and were in favour of the river route. Ian Preston told them that would cost twice as much as restoration on the original line and would bring little benefit to the village shops. The following year the council revealed its choice when it applied for planning permission to rebuild the canal through the centre of Slaithwaite along the original line. There were objections – but not as many as might have been expected – and permission was eventually granted.

It was nearly four years since I had first met Oldham planner John Billington to discuss a possible third MSC scheme on the canal. In February 1987 BW's Alex Thomson and I met him again this time with Bob Heycock, the council's MSC Agency Manager, and engineers from the council. At last they were ready for a scheme to start. HCS would pay the extra costs of materials and plant from the GMC grant as we were doing in Tameside. Treasurer Les Winnard arranged methods of accounting, billing and payment. The MSC and BW agreed to the scheme, starting in January 1988 on locks 18W-20W in Greenfield. The scheme would be supervised by George Cragg who had managed the council's scheme on the Rochdale Canal.

Stanley Clinton Davies, the European Commissioner for Transport, opened the Tameside Festival in 1987, supported by the largest VIP party yet seen with over seventy guests. The sun shone, the crowds flocked in and everything ran like clockwork until it was realised that the platform for the speakers had not been delivered. One was quickly constructed out of beer crates and an old tabletop. The list of invitees to the Huddersfield Festival that year included the Yorkshire Area Sports Council represented by Cyril Villiers. The council had been persuaded by Mike Thompson to give £40,000 to the Standedge Tunnel survey. Remembering his generosity to HCS as Mayor of Kirklees, Councillor Stanley Dawson was presented with a Festival plaque by Councillor George Speight at Lock 1E, which was named the Stanley Dawson Lock in appreciation.

1987 was not all good news. Although Bates's had built their new building in Huddersfield to allow for the canal, it would be some years before restoration reached here and the company was short of storage space. They applied for permission to build a wall around the area under the building and to use that space for storage. Kirklees refused planning permission and the company appealed. Witnesses at the public inquiry included thirteen-year-old Craig Watson, John Maynard's grandson, Kirklees planner John Miller and Mike Thompson representing HCS. So concerned was the council that Les Preece, the Chairman of the Council's Development and Technical Service Committee, also gave evidence. The Government Inspector rejected the appeal saying the development would increase the cost of restoration and jeopardise the whole through-restoration plan. A few days after that decision Stewart Sim, David Sumner, Brian Dice (Chief Executive, BW) and Malcolm Stakes (mining engineer, BW) took a trip through Standedge Tunnel, and they invited Gordon Bates, the chairman and managing director of Bates & Co., to show him that there was more to the canal. The trip took nearly three hours in the tunnel maintenance boat steered by long-standing BW employee (and friend of HCS) Fred Carter. A rock fall towards the Marsden end required a clamber into a side adit into the disused rail tunnel before boarding another boat beyond the fall.

Towards the end of the year *Benjamin Outram* was taken on a low-loader to Marsden where it was craned into the canal at Warehouse Hill. Harold Nield had plans for a boat of his own at Uppermill and *Benjie* would start trips in Marsden in 1988. Harold was soon operating *Pennine Moonraker* at Uppermill, winning a Tourist Board award for his efforts, and proving beyond doubt that the restored canal would attract investment. He operated *Pennine Moonraker* successfully for several years before passing the business on to John Lund.

Benjamin Outram below Lock 42E, Marsden. *(HCS)*

One of the conditions of the GMC grant was that BW sponsor an Act of Parliament to rescind the clause of the 1944 Act that made navigation illegal. On Tuesday 3 November 1987 members and officers of the local authorities, officers of BW, David Sumner and Mike Thompson visited the House of Commons to lobby members of both Houses of Parliament about a forthcoming Bill to rescind the Act. A display was put on in a committee room. Councillor Les Preece of Kirklees chaired the proceedings with a short presentation followed by lunch on the terrace. The British Waterways (No.2) Act subsequently received the Royal Assent on 29 July 1988. The important clause reads:

Subsection (1) (a) of Section 3 (Closing of Canals) of the Act of 1944 shall cease to apply to the relevant canals and the Board may permit their use for navigation.

This made it legal to navigate the canals abandoned by the LMS Railway in 1944 with the prior approval of BW. The Act had cost the local authorities, BW and HCS about £100,000 – but it was money well spent.

Mike Thompson had been meeting staff of the Department of the Environment, both in London and Manchester, for months to pave the way for applications for European Regional Development Fund grants. In January 1988 he submitted applications for the MSC work, the rebuilding of the Saddleworth bridges, Staley Wharf and the volunteer work at Diggle. These would be decided locally as part of the Mersey Basin Campaign, but the application for a grant towards the engineering study of Standedge Tunnel, and a leisure consultants study of the visitor centre at Tunnel End that he had submitted a few months earlier, would be decided in Brussels. It was a massive boost when that grant was approved towards the end of 1988. Of the £302,750 estimated cost half would come from Brussels with the rest from Kirklees, Tameside and Oldham Councils (£15,000 each), BW (£30,000) and £40,000 from the Yorkshire and Humberside Sports Council with HCS making up the difference. With the support given by the L&R Study we had been confident that the applications for actual work on the canal would be equally successful until we heard that the Treasury was limiting the amount for the voluntary sector, and this may go to one or more 'flagship' schemes.

Kirklees Council had also applied for European grants. In 1988 they learned that they were to get £165,000 for work over the years 1985 to 1989. This was the first large grant for work on the canal. We hoped it would set a precedent for our applications. Then the possibility of rebuilding the canal where it had been filled in alongside Hartshead power station came nearer. The power station was closed and demolished. The soon to be privatised Central Electricity Generating Board agreed with Tameside Council that a new sub-station would be off the route of the canal and BW and the generating board agreed on the transfer of the strip of land for the canal.

HCS increasingly needed a full-time employee beyond the staff at Tameside Canals as demands on the Society increased. Mike Thompson submitted an application under a Department of the Environment Special Grants Programme and we were offered £45,000 to be paid in instalments to 1991. We agreed a job specification and advertisements were placed in local and national papers. Seven people selected from ninety-five applicants were interviewed in August 1988 and Frank Smith, a former regular soldier, was appointed. He had ended his army career as a Warrant Officer, and had experience of manpower, planning, public relations, personnel and administration. His working brief was wide, covering administrative duties and liaison with anybody involved in the project. In fact it amounted to having to grow into the job and see how it developed.

Just as HCS gained new blood, we lost the surviving member of the original Committee when Bob Dewey resigned. He had a new job in Leicestershire. John Maynard attended Bob's last council meeting on 7 August 1988 to present him with a painting of the canal at Marsden. Without Bob's persistence and enthusiasm the Society might not have been formed. A few months later there were changes at BW when Regional Manager Stewart Sim was promoted

Left to right: Stephen Whitby, Michael Thompson and Frank Smith. *(HCS)*

and Derek Cochrane succeeded him. David Pyrah retired in 1989 too, which meant that Steve Whitby lost his unofficial engineering advisor.

In September 1988 the job creation schemes were thrown into disarray. The government replaced Community Programme with a new scheme, Employment Training (ET). The Manpower Services Commission became the Training Commission. ET was intended to address skill shortages for the long-term unemployed. It would provide on the job training combined with training by Colleges of Education or other approved educational establishments. All of the three MSC schemes continued but the approaches were different. Kirklees limited their scheme's exposure to ET by having twenty-two full-time staff plus a small number of trainees. The lockgate workshop at Linthwaite was separated out as Concrete and Timber Services Ltd with council officers and members as directors. The company would sell lockgates and produce timber footbridges, picnic tables etc. to be self-financing. Ernest Aitken, the Site Foreman, would take on more responsibility as Ian Preston spent time managing the company and finding outside work. Similarly the Oldham Council scheme, that had begun work on locks 18W and 19W (Royal George Locks) in Greenfield a few months previously, continued but the council would struggle to make ET work.

Tameside Canals had just been awarded a Civic Trust UK2000 kitemark for the high standard of work. We had employed more than 900 people, many of whom went into full-time employment. We were worried about our ability to manage a training scheme and preferred Tameside Canals to subcontract to another scheme manager. The obvious choice was to sub-contract to Tameside Council, but the council's arrangements had relied on independent operators like Tameside Canals. They needed time to adjust to a training regime. We had to look elsewhere and decided that Tameside Canals would act as a sub-contractor to J. Jarvis & Sons plc, a national building contractor who were setting up an Employment Training Division. Tameside Canals would manage its own programme of work. Jarvis would provide administrative support, training packages, negotiations with trade unions, and safety advice. Steve Whitby and John McLouglin continued with fourteen other employees to provide for up to 200 trainees. The new regime required a range of training choices. To give the operation a chance of being a viable business the Board of Tameside Canals decided that, in addition to building skills, we would offer training in computing and office administration skills. Bob Gough was appointed to support this; he had been self-employed, running a small computer training scheme, which attracted him to us in the first place, but he also had a degree in Botany and Geology and a PhD in civil engineering. His doctoral thesis had been related to drought stresses in vegetation. He could understand and talk the language of ecologists – crucial in Tameside with its SSSI. The plan for 1988-19889 was to complete Lock Nos 9W-11W, begin work on locks 15W-17W, carry out dredging and continue with towpath and landscaping work. Work was to move to locks 15W-17W because we could not work on Lock 12W. A landslip of the adjoining disused railway embankment required

Tameside Canals workers clearing the lock chamber of infill material. Lock 10W. *(HCS)*

extensive engineering and geotechnical surveys. Rather than just skip a lock, it seemed logical to move immediately across the district boundary from the Oldham scheme. In the autumn of 1988, in recognition of his help, Alex Thomson was appointed to the Board as were Steve Whitby (becoming managing director), HCS Vice Chairman Trevor Ellis and local industrialist Neville Kenyon.

Work on the canal stopped. Setting up training programmes took precedence. With a full-time restoration workforce Kirklees soon restarted in the Colne Valley, but Tameside Canals struggled to make progress and the Oldham Council scheme ground to a halt. Employment Training was not suited to canal restoration. The benefit of providing employment for large numbers of people had been crucial to being accepted to work on the canal by BW; now an equally large number of people also had to be educated. We rented extra floorspace on an industrial estate. City & Guilds courses were offered with day release training at Tameside College in brickwork and blockwork, carpentry and joinery, and general building skills. Back at the office in Mossley Road computer literacy, word processing, bookeeping and clerical skills were taught. The meeting room was filled with computers. Few of the unemployed saw much future in being a general building operative so it was difficult to re-start work on the canal. We solved this in the same way as Kirklees had – by taking on extra staff. Community Programme had paid the wages, administration and accommodation costs, bought two vans and a car needed to run the scheme, and some of the plant and materials costs. We paid for large items such as lock gates or stone to rebuild a lock chamber. With ET all that was received was a payment for each trainee. ET would only subsidise the restoration programme if tasks provided a vehicle for training, and if the training operation made a profit. In the first few months that worked, but only because so much effort was diverted to training that hardly any work took place on the canal.

The situation with the Oldham Council scheme was even worse. They could not get trainees in relatively affluent Saddleworth. By June 1989 we had bills of £58,000 for expensive hired plant which was standing idle. The council was understandably reluctant to admit failure but in August 1989, after nearly a year of little progress, it was agreed that the only solution was for Tameside Canals to take on the total west-side programme; we could bring in trainees from further down the valley. In recognition of this change Tameside Canals was re-named HCS Restoration Ltd. A separate company was set up to manage training, HCS Training Ltd. Because of the crucial importance of training, David Sumner took on the role of chairman. Frank Ruffley continued as chairman of HCS Restoration. Steve Whitby would be managing director of both companies. Management on site at HCS Restoration would be the responsibility of Manager John McLouglin and Supervisor Malcolm Braddock with Ken Dyball as manager of HCS Training.

Tameside Canals and the Jarvis operation had worked well together, but in September 1989 the Training Commission suggested that HCS Restoration was large enough to stand on its own feet. With experience we knew that was possible. We continued with a total of twenty-one staff – nine to work on the canal. The first year of the training operation had contributed about £50,000 towards restoration work and trainees had done £20,000 worth of work on the canal, but the cost of work planned from September 1989 to August 1990 was around £250,000. It was hoped that HCS Training Ltd would make a profit, but the cost of running the scheme was high and the risks remained significant. Further investment in vehicles was needed, with HCS Restoration buying a Leyland DAF 400 crew cab truck with a crane for loading and unloading. Progress was again being made on the canal with rapid headway on locks 15W and 17W as work concentrated on the canal between Locks 15W and 17W (in Tameside) and Locks 18W and 20W (in Oldham).

At the end of 1989 Ian Preston's team completed the thirty-seventh lock – the halfway stage. Restoration was progressing on both sides of the hills, but at an increasing cost. Still we were no longer committed to the dreaded hydraulic paddle gear. It was not as reliable as BW

Andy Sharp pointing the locktail bridge below the restored Lock 16W, Mossley. *(HCS)*

The restored Lock 17W and Division Bridge.
(Kathryn Gibson)

HCS Restoration staff pose at Lock 16W, including long-term members John Harrison (left), Andy Sharp (fourth left), John McLouglin (seventh left), John Francis (ninth left), and Ken Williams (tenth left) with office staff Steve Whitby, Paula Mclouglin and Bob Gough on the right. *(HCS)*

hoped and they raised no real objections when the Society decided to use the traditional Telford-designed off-side mounted paddle gear at Diggle, and traditional Trent & Mersey Canal gear elsewhere. It was not historically accurate to use that design from another canal, but Harold Nield and the boat crews who struggled with the Huddersfield gear at Uppermill wanted no more of that.

In October 1989 Ove Arup presented their report on Standedge Tunnel. Writing in *Pennine Link,* Glyn Walton of Ove Arup said that, although there were places where unlined sections of roof were so unstable that 'anyone who was likely to sneeze would be told to man the site office', the tunnel was in remarkably good shape for its age. A substantial amount of debris and 20,000 cubic metres of silt would have to be removed, but the lined sections of tunnel were reasonable – which was a relief as 60% of the tunnel was lined. The eight remaining construction shafts were surveyed using closed circuit television cameras. Restoration of the tunnel would cost between £5 million and £8 million depending on the scale of work carried out. At the same time we were presented with the report on what they called the Standedge Experience by L&R Leisure. A visitor centre was proposed at each end of the tunnel. At Diggle this would interpret the weather (a good idea that has yet to find its time). In the BW warehouse at Tunnel End the story of Pennine transport would be interpreted and there would be a twenty-five-minute trip into the tunnel. Before we could consider how this was to be paid for, a lot of work was needed by BW, especially by mining engineer Malcolm Stakes, to decide which repairs were essential and which could be left undone or tackled later.

To complete all of the canal was going to need large grants. The big problems at Stalybridge, Slaithwaite, Huddersfield or even Standedge Tunnel might be eligible for grants designed for economic or environmental regeneration, but applications for those grants could not be contemplated until the straightforward lock restoration had been completed, and these lengths of the canal were disrupted by lowered bridges. The GMC legacy had been intended to help with some of these but the lock restoration and dredging was becoming very expensive and there was no obvious source of grants for the bridges apart from the European applications. Despite continual lobbying and prompting by Mike Thompson, there was still no sign of a decision on these. The small group of David Sumner, Trevor Ellis, Bob Maycock, Brian Minor, Mike Thompson, Steve Whitby, Les Winnard and I met to form the Construction Group with the idea of bringing more brain power to these issues. I was appointed Chair of the Group. Well-known volunteer Eric Crosland and senior local authority engineer Ken Wright soon joined the group.

In February 1990 Mike Thompson and I attended another meeting with the Department of the Environment in Manchester in connection with our applications for European money. They were still intent on offering the main part of their voluntary sector budget to one or two 'flagship' schemes. We were asking for £317,000 for the basic work of HCS Restoration and were no longer hopeful of anything more. In the end, by midsummer, we received £65,000 – a lot less than we applied for, but it was 20% of the grants paid to the voluntary sector in the Mersey Basin area. Undeterred we submitted a bid for further European money, prepared by Mike Thompson and Steve Whitby with a lot of help from local authority engineers, for Manns Wharf and Frenches Bridges, Locks 18W-20W, dredging and environmental work.

In April 1990 the government again changed the rules. The Training Commission ended ET contracts with one month's notice. New contracts were offered. Kirklees was able to continue, but we were offered only seventy trainees and a reduced fee for each trainee. HCS Training would lose at least £40,000 per year. We met Training Commission staff, with support from British Waterways and the local authorities, but no improvement was forthcoming. The boundaries had changed. We now had to deal with the Central Manchester office rather than the Stockport office of the Commission. National builders had training facilities in Manchester. With access to Construction Industry Training Board grants they could carry out all training in-house. HCS Training had to buy in courses from Tameside College. We could not compete. On 22 May 1990 I chaired a joint meeting of the Construction Group and the Boards of HCS Training Ltd and HCS Restoration Ltd. We could not continue with a business venture that was certain to make a substantial loss. Five people, including Training Manager Ken Dyball, would be made redundant. That would leave a nine-person restoration team working for HCS Restoration under Steve Whitby. Bob Gough stayed doing computing work and because he could talk the language of English Nature, as the Nature Conservancy Council had become. It was a sad day. Staff who had been employed by the Society since the early days of the Community Programme left and the Society ended its direct involvement with Employment Training.

Steve Whitby had kept his contacts with the local authority training agencies and before the decision to close the training company he had established that they would provide trainees on placement. Work experience was not easy to find in Tameside or Oldham. Overheads were cut by ending the rental of workshop units for training and staff costs were reduced, but the annual wage and running costs would be around £130,000 before allowing for materials and plant costs, and we lost the opportunity to make any profit from training. There was no choice but to eat into capital or close down altogether – and that was not a realistic option, or work might never start again.

On 3 and 4 June 1990 thirty-five boats made the ascent through locks 1W-3W after the official party performed the tape-cutting ceremony, as the very first part of the canal to connect with the main system was finally opened. The Tameside Canal Boat Trust's trip boat *Greater Manchester*, which would soon be operated by HCS boat crews providing trips from Portland Basin, carried the VIPs. Lock 1W was opened by Glyn Ford MEP, Lock 2W by John Tavaré, Chairman of the Mersey Basin Campaign, and Lock 3W by Ken Goodwin, Chairman of the IWA. Dobcross Band, including Steve Whitby on cornet, welcomed *Greater Manchester* at Lock 1W. Although formally open this length of canal would not see much use for some time. There was nowhere to turn so a trip up the canal meant difficult reversing.

The Society held the usual Huddersfield and Tameside Festivals that year as well as the sales caravan attending the IWA National Rally and other events. The first commercial load for many a year was carried on the canal on the Friday morning prior to the Tameside Festival. Mailbox International, manufacturers of litterbins, loaned bins to the Festival Committee each year. With their premises just above Lock 3W the collection could now be by water. The Ashton Packet Boat Co. provided an old wooden working boat *Joel*. With nowhere to turn the muscle of the lads from HCS Restoration had to be enlisted to help *Joel* reverse to the site, but the bins were delivered. Schools and other groups enjoyed trips at Marsden on *Benjamin Outram,* but the jet propulsion unit was now so totally unreliable that most trips were horse-drawn by 'Tanner'. Alwyn Ogborn had taken over as editor of *Pennine Link* and an A4-size *Tunnel Survey Special* was much in demand. Although HCS had more members than ever before, co-ordination was difficult. The Promotions Group was formed bringing together volunteers from the festivals, the boat crews and the sales, press and publicity activities of the Society. Alwyn Ogborn, Brian Minor, Jo Young and Jack Carr at different times chaired the group – the largely unsung heroes of the restoration campaign who put in a huge number of hours organising events, manning the sales stand and, in Jo's case, spending untold hours keeping the Society's membership records in good order – not to mention appearing in traditional boatwoman's costume whenever possible.

Then tragedy struck. HCS Restoration had taken over the Oldham Council project and completed restoration of the Royal George Locks; lock numbers 18W & 19W. The site was being cleared when trainee Keith Jackson died following an accident with an excavator at the site entrance. The excavator driver was experienced and familiar with working around the

Re-opening Locks 1W-3W, June 1990. The Mayor watches as *Greater Manchester* rises in Lock 1W before Glyn Ford MEP cuts the tape. *(Trevor Ellis)*

Sue McBride and flowers at the opening of the second exhibition, Tunnel End Cottages, Marsden, 8 September 1990. Sue designed both exhibitions here, which showed the benefits of restoration of the canal to the many visitors to the cottages. *(David Finnis)*

canal, as HCS Restoration had hired plant and drivers from his employers regularly, and there was a watchman keeping an eye out to ensure that nobody came too near. Health and Safety was almost an obsession to Steve Whitby and the full-time staff and was regularly discussed at Board meetings. That a site was safe was especially important when sites were populated by trainees who may not be used to the dangers of a building site, particularly a site with water and deep lock chambers.

I can only speak for myself on this, and I find it difficult to set down how I felt without it sounding trite – a feeling of compassion towards Mr Jackson and his family, a difficulty in comprehending what must be going through the minds of the excavator driver and the watchman, and tremendous sympathy for Frank Ruffley, Steve Whitby, John McLoughlin and the others on site and in the office who somehow had to deal with the tragedy and carry on. Frank Ruffley and Steve Whitby dealt with the situation in as professional a manner as they could; other members of the Board of HCS Restoration were rightly told the misguided sympathy of amateur directors could do nothing to help. Frank Smith unofficially named Lock 18W the Keith Jackson lock on any maps issued from the HCS office afterwards.

On the weekend of 8 and 9 September 1990 a new exhibition at Tunnel End Cottages, again designed by Sue McBride, was opened by the Mayor of Kirklees, Councillor Tom Donovan. The exhibition and alterations to the building cost £30,000, provided by Kirklees, HCS and the National Trust. The event was linked with a festival, the principal organiser being David Finnis, now the Marsden Moor Warden for the National Trust. Towards the end of the year the boat crews were reliant on *No.2*, at Marsden, for which a new outboard motor had been purchased. They were also running trips at Portland Basin with the Tameside Canal Boat Trust's *Greater Manchester. Stan* was at Mossley Road looking very forlorn after being sunk by vandals at Marsden. *Benjamin Outram* was advertised for sale, being out of the water at BW's Marsden yard. A new purpose-built boat was being designed for the top pound at Marsden but a cleaned up and repaired *Stan* and *No.2* would soldier on for most of the next year.

Left: The Kirklees scheme moved rapidly down the valley. Lock 8E at Milnsbridge, July 1991. *(HCS)*

Below: Traditional mechanical paddle gear fitted to Lock 18W, with the 'pepperpot' used by HCS Restoration to cover the air vents to paddle culverts. *(HCS)*

The new Whiteley Street bridge, Milnsbridge, 1991. *(HCS)*

Actor and singer David Essex with HCS Boat Officer Robert Maycock at the launch of *Marsden Shuttle* at Tunnel End, Marsden, 10 October 1991. *(HCS)*

By December 1990 forty-eight of the original seventy-four locks were restored and ten miles of canal dredged. Kirklees was employing twenty-two full-time staff and a few trainees, and spending at a rate of £200,000 a year. The canal was restored between Tunnel End and Lock 25E above Slaithwaite; between Slaithwaite and Milnsbridge locks 9E to 20E were operational. HCS Restoration had restored locks 1W-3W and 9W-11W, and dredged the canal between Whitelands Road and Bayley Street, and from Grove Road to Scout Tunnel; below Uppermill locks 15W-20W were now operational through Greenfield to Mossley and work had moved on to locks 13W and 14W in Mossley. Oldham and Tameside Councils agreed to continue paying the £45,000 transitional grant paid after the demise of the county council because of the difficulties created by having to withdraw from ET. Even with this, however, the Society's reserves were down to £893,661 by the end of 1990. Spending at that rate could not continue if HCS was to keep a large capital sum as seed corn for major projects.

Kirklees Council was near the end of its lock restoration and dredging programme but they hit a series of problems in 1991, coming across locks that needed the sort of major rebuilding HCS Restoration was used to on the west-side. The council had, however, rebuilt Whiteley Street bridge, Milnsbridge, because it did not meet the standard for increased vehicle weights. That removed the prop in the canal blocking the way into the lock directly above the bridge. There was more good news in 1991 when Tameside Council decided to spend £50,000 on the enlargement of a sewer to allow the removal of pipes on the route of Staley Wharf, and the council's engineers were designing the new bridge required at Bayley Street.

On Sunday 20 October 1991 there was an enthusiastic turn-out at Tunnel End to witness the launch of the new trip boat *Marsden Shuttle* by singer and actor David Essex, making the news in the local press and television. David had agreed to become a patron of the Society,

Scout Tunnel with the new handrail fixed to the towpath *(HCS)*

along with *Last of the Summer Wine* television actress Thora Hird and environmentalist Professor David Bellamy. He played the part of a lock-keeper in a popular television series *The River* and tried his hand steering the new boat which was purpose-built to provide a shuttle service between the top lock at Marsden and Tunnel End carrying only twelve passengers – so being short enough to turn in the width of the canal, and avoiding the need for skippers to have a licence. Having the boat built was frustrating as delivery dates slipped and the firm building it went bankrupt. It was finished by Kevin Wadsworth of Warble Narrow Boats at Hyde nearby on the Peak Forest Canal.

On the west-side the HCS Restoration Ltd workforce should have been dredging in Mossley after completing locks 13W and 14W, and planning to move to the Diggle flight of locks. Although planning permission for a site to tip dredgings alongside Milton Mills, Mossley, was received in March, consideration of the application for a Waste Disposal Licence was slow. That caused a temporary delay providing time for small tasks that were tending to be left with only a small workforce – towpath and washwall work and the provision of a handrail to the towpath through Scout Tunnel. We thought a new source of grant-aid might prove very significant and Mike Thompson was beginning discussions with the Department of the Environment. That would only apply to tasks not yet started, so no further lock was started in 1991. Our workforce turned to help the volunteers at Diggle. A welcome bi-product of this was that, after the heavy costs of 1990, HCS spent only £6,472 more than the interest on the capital sum in 1991. It had been a rocky ride but the possibility of grants might make the financial future less uncertain.

11 Into the Premier League

HCS Restoration had paid for the restoration of locks 13W-20W with financial help from Oldham and Tameside Councils and a small European grant. Keeping the company afloat was eating into the Society's reserves. I wished that the government's Derelict Land Grant scheme applied to waterway restoration. Unlike other grants it covered all the costs, but these grants had been for reclamation of dereliction left behind by industry and mining or to create jobs on derelict sites. In May 1991 the Department of the Environment began to include schemes that restored derelict land for environmental improvement that enhanced an area for investment. What more obvious candidate than a derelict canal whose restoration would have significant environmental and economic benefits?

Even better, negotiations in the Oldham and Tameside districts would be with the Department's Manchester office where Mike Thompson already had a good working relationship. After Mike had had several preliminary meetings, I joined him and Steve Whitby to meet the Department of the Environment officers with planners Nick Andrews (Oldham) and Steve Hughes (Tameside) and Tameside engineer Peter Rawson in October 1991. It seemed very promising. A visit to the canal was arranged. With David Sumner and Ken Wright to beef up the HCS representation, we showed them the canal from Diggle to Stalybridge. In one of those moments that remain in your mind forever, over coffee in the HCS office, Tim Routledge, who led the government officers, said that everything they had seen could be eligible for grant. I knew then that all of the canal would be restored.

Department of the Environment visit to the west side of the canal. Local authority staff present were Tameside Council engineer Peter Rawson (left), Tameside Council planner Stephen Hughes (fourth left) and Oldham Council planner, Nicholas Andrews (seventh left). HCS members present were Ken Wright (fifth left), David Sumner (sixth left) and Keith Gibson (second from right). Timothy Routledge (third from right) led the DoE delegation, and the HCS contingent was made up by Stephen Whitby who took the photograph. *(HCS)*

Steve Whitby and Tameside engineer Peter Rawson burnt the midnight oil preparing a programme of work for approval by both councils and the Joint Committee. The councils would have to submit the grant applications. Oldham and Tameside had welcomed our help but it seemed harder in Kirklees. The regional office of the Department of the Environment had different priorities, and Calderdale Council was first off the mark by submitting their scheme to open up the blockage at Tuel Lane in Sowerby Bridge on the Rochdale Canal.

Meanwhile the HCS Restoration team was concentrating on towpath repairs between Greenfield and Mossley and building a slipway at Wool Road helped by small grants from charitable trusts, a grant of £5,000 from the Civic Trust and an impressive £5,000 worth of materials from Stalybridge Rotary Club. The Waste Disposal Licence for the dredgings tip at Mossley was received and the site prepared to receive spoil from the canal alongside. Employment Action, another job creation scheme, came along in 1992. No training was involved. Employers provided work and the Government paid participants £10 a week over any welfare benefits they received. Additional workers were useful for labour intensive work repairing washwalls and towpaths. We gratefully accepted an offer of up to thirty-five workers. The volunteers continued working at Diggle, completing work on Lock 31W. That was marked by a small ceremony on 24 January 1992 as the fiftieth lock to be restored on the canal – only another twenty-four to go.

We had fallen into a pattern of holding a Construction Group meeting immediately before the HCS Restoration Board meeting. In February 1992 HCS Council decided to merge the Construction Group with HCS Restoration. Frank Ruffley resigned as Chairman of HCS Restoration, I resigned as Chairman of the Construction Group, and I was appointed Chairman of HCS Restoration Ltd. David Sumner presented Frank with an original watercolour of Portland Basin. Frank remained a director. He had successfully chaired HCS Restoration and its predecessors, Tameside Canals Ltd and the Tameside Canals Development Association, for eight years but he no longer felt able to continue in a leading role. Ken Wright was appointed deputy chairman in May.

In Kirklees the lock restoration and dredging work should have been complete by March 1992, but Lock 24E and the pound between there and the Slaithwaite infilled section remained untouched. With a contribution from HCS the council could keep the staff employed for a few months more, but it was soon apparent that it would take far too long to resolve the complex problems of lock 24E. The seventeen staff remaining were made redundant. Concrete & Timber Services Ltd, the council-owned workshop at Linthwaite, was sold to scheme manager Ian Preston. The company still trades, although in different premises. Ian Preston, Site Manager Ernest Aitken and the team had restored thirty-six locks. The canal had been dredged, washwalls rebuilt, and a decent towpath provided between Marsden and Slaithwaite, and from Slaithwaite through Linthwaite, Golcar and Milnsbridge to Longroyd Bridge. It was a difficult time for the team to be facing redundancy, although some were re-deployed within the council. The council had spent £1,223,500 together with £126,500 from the former County Council, £165,500 from the European Regional Development Fund and £125,000 from BW. The Training Commission, and its predecessor the Manpower Services Commission, had provided £240,000 for plant and materials plus about £2,000,000 in labour costs, giving a total spend of £3,880,000 on the canal. The incomplete work would be taken over by HCS Restoration – for the first time working east of the Pennines. Both walls of lock 24E required some rebuilding. Like Lock 2W the bridge below the lock had been widened over the tail of the lock, but reducing the width of the bridge here would prevent access by modern vehicles to the industrial premises of Elon Crowther's. A guillotine, or vertically lifting, gate could just be squeezed in to the space available and had been decided on as the best solution. To pay for this we applied for a Derelict Land Grant, although as a voluntary sector applicant we could only receive 80% rather than the 100% awarded to local authorities.

Our second application for European money for work on the canal bore fruit with a grant of £27,000 in 1992 made retrospectively for work on Locks 18W-20W. And Tameside Council

Frank Ruffley holds in *Greater Manchester* at the Tameside Canals Festival. *(HCS)*

received £36,000 towards the sewer diversion at Staley Wharf and for work HCS Restoration had carried out at lock 14W. The Society had raised another £27,000 from its efforts to bridge the funding gap in 1991 after an appeal letter from Thora Hird – from members donations and charitable trusts, local and national businesses, and from the Civic Trust.

An application was submitted for further European money for the Transhipment Warehouse adjacent to Wool Road Basin, Dobcross. This was the terminus of the western part of the canal between 1799 and 1811 when goods were taken to Marsden by packhorse. The warehouse is the last remaining building here and listed as of architectural or historic interest. It had been the loading shed for Stonebottom Mill, now converted to dwellings, behind the warehouse across the River Tame, but the name reflected the historic importance of the basin. A stone-built shelter whose stone slate roof overhangs the canal, it had been rescued from dereliction and the roof re-slated by the Saddleworth Historical Society. It would provide a meeting room serving local needs and the Tame Valley Warden Service would pay rent for use on sufficient days to make this a viable proposition. BW, who owned the building, would lease it to HCS at a rent reflecting the likely small income. Architecture & Design Partnership, an architectural practice with a track record of sensitive conversion work, was appointed but instructed only to prepare sketch plans until the result of the grant application was known. This was categorised as a second priority scheme so a grant looked unlikely, but Steve Whitby was looking into other sources of money and Russell Earnshaw, the architect, agreed a sketch design with Oldham Council.

BW had prepared a brief for further study of the construction shafts and the ventilation requirements for navigation of Standedge Tunnel. Oldham Council's application for a Derelict Land Grant of £150,000 was approved quickly and Ove Arups were appointed to do this work, but none of the applications for work on the canal had yet been through all stages of approval. Until grants were approved work at HCS Restoration was managed on a week by week basis. The likelihood of change was constant. The Government had issued a Consultation Paper setting out plans for an urban regeneration agency which, amongst other things, would take over the Derelict Land Grant programme. We feared that the changes to the grant regime might be reversed putting the emphasis back on schemes that directly created jobs.

A sponsored walk, Toepath '91, had been organised in October 1991 but the eighty-seven people who walked between Marsden and Longroyd Bridge to raise £1,400 was less than hoped for, and far less took part in Toepath '92. The days of sponsored walks seemed to be over. The Festivals continued. In 1992 Kathy Staff (Nora Batty, of locally filmed *Last of the Summer Wine* fame), and all the Department of the Environment officials we knew, were invited to Ashton – recognising those who did the work as well as those at the top. The 1992 Summer Fair in Marsden was graced with glorious weather. *No.2* was transformed into a pirate galleon with furled up sails and gun ports complete with Captian Hook and his crew; HCS stalwarts Ronnie Rose and Ian France. Public trips were provided every weekend at Marsden on *Marsden Shuttle* and at Ashton on *Greater Manchester*. Boat officer Bob Maycock shared his responsibilities with other crew members. Peter Ruffley dealt with schools and organisations. Ian France and David Muir kept the boats on the move and Alan Knott had the thankless task of arranging crew rotas. Changes in the law meant that skippers of *Greater Manchester* required a Department of Transport Boatman's Licence. Training was organised and the tester came to Portland Basin. By midsummer 1992 HCS had twelve licensed skippers. *Pennine Link*, now a glossy quarterly, was again voted the best canal society magazine in 1992 by the IWA awards judges. The magazine made quite a splash when actor Bill Owen, known to television viewers as Compo from the *Last of the Summer Wine* series, was signed on as the society's 2000th member. Bill was as good as his word when he offered to help, being willing to turn out for all sorts of events, provided it did not clash with filming schedules. It is a great tragedy that he did not live to see the canal open.

HCS was still keeping HCS Restoration solvent while we waited for grant approvals. Nobody disagreed when John Sully, the former County Councillor appointed to the council of HCS and now Treasurer of the Society, said that never again should we keep people employed for an indefinite period without any guarantee of future income. At last, two and

HCS member number 2000, actor Bill Owen, with Alwyn Ogborn, and Brian Minor with his grandson. Jo Young hides behind Bill Owen. *(HCS)*

The Transhipment warehouse, Dobcross. *(HCS)*

a half years after we pulled out of Employment Training, the first Derelict Land Grant application was approved for dredging work, washwall and towpath repairs between Lock 13W in Mossley and Division Bridge. Tameside Council gave the contract to HCS Restoration. Work started almost immediately using more modern hired British Waterways plant rather than our own much slower dredger *Norwood*. So by the end of 1992 we could look forward to a period of relative stability in the financing of HCS Restoration. This first Derelict Land Grant scheme was soon complete and the second phase of major dredging work between Lock 12W and Lock 13W in Mossley started. Then Oldham Council received approval of the most important grant for HCS Restoration, the Diggle flight of locks, at an anticipated cost of £803,000. Work would start in November 1993. The completion of the seven locks in this contract would bring our workforce up to locks 31W and 32W which were being restored by volunteers which were almost complete.

There was unexpected news immediately after Christmas 1992 when our application for European money towards the conversion of the Transhipment Warehouse was approved after all. Oldham Council confirmed that their 1991 grant of £23,000 to the Society, the last under the transitional grant arrangements after the demise of GMC, could be spent on this project, and Steve Whitby negotiated donations from Charitable Trusts. Architecture & Design quickly produced detailed drawings and submitted applications to the council for permission. When these were approved it was a case of 'all hands to the pumps' because the grant had a tight spending deadline. Our workforce and subcontractors were seriously extended completing work in time, but the finished building was to a standard appropriate for this Listed Building. The cost to the Society of the £52,000 project was slightly more than £4,000, and money well spent in promoting the recreational use and restoration of the canal. Yet there was a row in HCS Council and speculation about the cost of the scheme. Some members did not grasp the significance of the grants to the scheme, or that our staff had worked wonders to complete the work in a matter of weeks. The warehouse was officially opened by local Councillor Brian Mather. HCS Council member Ken Wright, who would act as caretaker of the renovated warehouse, led the HCS team. One of the first events in September 1993 was a barbecue sponsored by suppliers to HCS Restoration to thank all those involved in the running of the Society's committees and sub-groups.

In April 1993 the last of the so useful trainees from the Employment Action programme left. The scheme was being replaced by a new scheme, Training for Work. That required participants to achieve qualifications. We would not divert effort and staff to training again. For twelve months HCS Restoration staff had been the only people working on the canal until Oldham Council let the first of the Derelict Land Grant-funded bridge rebuilding contracts to J. Fisk & Co. for a new bridge at Manns Wharf, Greenfield. Work started in May 1993.

Before work started at Diggle, the HCS Restoration team moved on to Lock 24E at Slaithwaite. Both walls needed rebuilding almost from bottom water level, and Wilde & Partners of Stockport, who had advised us on engineering matters before, were entrusted with designing the guillotine lockgate. A local company, Tinker Engineering of Middleton, Oldham – whose boss, Ron Tinker, was a prominent member of the Rochdale Canal Society – was contracted to manufacture the gate. This was not the only work being carried out by the Society east of the Pennines. Our tender had been accepted by Kirklees for Derelict Land Grant-funded towpath and washwall work and the repair of Lock 1E in Huddersfield. A grant had also been offered to allow the removal of the causeway across the canal at the University (as the Polytechnic had now become) which prevented access to Lock 1E from Aspley Basin. Work by HCS Restoration throughout the length of the canal meant expensive minibus hire. That, plus the fact that John Sully recommended it was financially prudent to change our truck, led to us buying two new vehicles to add to the fleet – a Leyland DAF 200 minibus and a similar, but larger, 400 truck with a crew cab. We did not keep the minibus for long. Despite alarms and security lights it was stolen from our yard, and replaced by a long wheelbase Land Rover that could pull the new caravan that volunteers were taking to events on a weekend. Something was said about the skin of a rice pudding concerning the minibus! The HCS dredger *Norwood*, a butty and a mud hopper were sold in June 1993, and the fleet of more modern BW vessels that had been hired was bought for £20,000 – the dredger *Pollard*, the appropriately-named tug *Ashton*, a discharge crane and two mud hoppers.

By the summer of 1993 the lock chamber at Lock 24E had been rebuilt and a new headgate fitted. Ken Wright, Steve Whitby and Neil Morton of Wilde & Partners visited the River Great Ouse to inspect guillotine lock gates. Ken Wright wrote in *Pennine Link* that 'without waving one's arms about, describing such a gate is not easy,' and more worryingly that 'the experts say they never work first time.' The National Rivers Authority kindly gave them engineering drawings, and Neil Morton designed a guillotine gate – but it would cost more than we first thought. Additional Derelict Land Grants were approved in Kirklees directly below this lock. The council gave the contracts to HCS Restoration. This involved dredging the canal between Locks 23E and 24E, and restoring Lock 23E and the short length of canal below connecting to the culvert through Slaithwaite. Further down the canal in Huddersfield a developer was interested in the site of the now demolished Haigh's Mill immediately above the blockage at Seller's Engineers. Derelict Land Grant of £300,000 was offered to reconstruct the infilled canal if a complete package for the whole site was forthcoming. Meanwhile HCS Restoration had started work transforming Lock 1E into an operating lock. Commercial Street bridge was painted and the canal dredged between there and lock 1E. Then Huddersfield University joined Kirklees to remove the temporary causeway across the canal below the lock, with work to start early in 1994 on the £177,000 contract that had been awarded to Morrison Construction. A new footbridge would replace the causeway.

On Friday 3 September 1993 a presentation was given by Alan Turner and Keith Sego of consulting engineers Ove Arup on the ventilation of Standedge Tunnel. They had studied airflows in the tunnel. It was subject to invasion by fumes as trains in the railway tunnel pushed air into the canal tunnel via the adits, but these were immediately sucked out again via the next adit as the train passed. Apart from that, air movement in the tunnel was very limited.

HCS Restoration working east of the Pennines. Dredging between Locks 1E and 2E, Huddersfield, June 1993. *(HCS)*

The new footbridge linking the two sides of the Huddersfield University campus across the arm of the Huddersfield Broad Canal leading to the Huddersfield Narrow Canal, 1994. (HCS)

Exhaust gases from a diesel-powered boat would drift at the same speed as the boat, staying with the boat through the tunnel, with the air becoming increasingly poisonous especially if more than one boat was in the tunnel. Unless the air was purged from the tunnel and fresh air brought in, internal combustion engines would be dangerous. Fans could purge the air – probably with self-closing doors to the adits so that they were not moving air in the railway tunnels – but they would have to move a very large mass of air in a tunnel this long. That would be very expensive and would make the tunnel noisy, windy and dusty. An electric tug service seemed to be necessary. This would have an added benefit of being able to dovetail with the timing of an electric trip boat into the tunnel. If Derelict Land Grant had stayed with the Department of the Environment, grants may have followed this presentation, but the government was pressing ahead with plans for English Partnerships as the new urban regeneration agency was to be called, and BW would need months to prepare tender documents for repairs that would be varied and complex to describe.

Since we heard that the government intended passing the Derelict Land Grant scheme to English Partnerships we had been concerned about the future of these grants. As the deadline for that changeover approached, the Department of the Environment advised the local authorities to submit a combined bid for the canal to English Partnerships, setting out all the work required, the total cost and a timetable for complete restoration. Entitled *Completing the Restoration of the Huddersfield Narrow Canal – A Bid for Resources*, this was produced, after much coming and going of local authority planners and engineers to the HCS office, by Steve Whitby and Bob Gough with text provided by the local authorities. The total cost came out at £23 million to complete the canal in 2003. A deputation from the Joint Committee chaired by David Sumner attended the House of Commons in March 1994 to launch the bid. David outlined the progress and spoke about the benefits showing canalside developments that had taken place because of restoration of the waterway. The time was right for a co-ordinated approach to final restoration and we were looking for support from members of both houses for our bid to English Partnerships. *Canal & Riverboat* magazine commented, 'Only HCS would launch a major fund-raising appeal to complete the canal, launch it in the Houses of Parliament, and expect to get the lot!'

The launch of the 'Bid for Resources', Houses of Parliament, March 1994. Left to Right: David Sumner, Councillor George Speight, Robert Sheldon MP and Geoffrey Dickens MP. *(HCS)*

HCS Restoration working on the derelict engine house at Redbrook, Standedge. *(HCS)*

We are getting ahead of the story. Back in 1993 HCS Restoration repaired and re-pointed the listed Red Brook engine house on Standedge at a cost of around £38,000 for BW, and very demanding as it required working to standards set by English Heritage. It took people away from Diggle where work had started and the loss of job creation or training participants to do straightforward tasks was delaying work. Then the Community Action Programme was announced. Our old friends at Jarvis Employment Training gained the contract to manage the scheme in the Oldham area. We agreed to provide up to fifty work places. Participants would work eighteen hours per week. We received £40 per week for each one less a supervision fee paid to Jarvis's and had to provide them with three hours of jobsearch training. We could cope with that, and it was a relief to have people to replace the Employment Action participants.

In extreme weather conditions before Christmas 1993 the off-side wall of Lock 24E collapsed into the lock, taking the section that had been rebuilt with it. Our engineers (Ken Wright and consultant Neil Morton of Wilde & Partners) and Neil Maxwell of BW took a while to establish the cause. Eventually, almost a year later in November 1994, work began to rebuild the wall. Drainage pipes were incorporated behind it to ensure that floodwater could not wash out the material behind the wall and cause a further collapse. As the collapse was not the result of any negligence on HCS Restoration's part, additional grant was paid.

The 1993 Tameside Festival expanded to include a Festival of Dance. *Pennine Link* editor Alwyn Ogborn again won the IWA award for the best canal society magazine. Frank Smith, who was finding his role as administrator, minute taker, speaker to schools, chambers of trade etc., took an interest in helping boat crews gain even more boatman's licences with twenty-five qualified skippers, including two ladies, by the summer of 1994. *Stan* was honourably retired, being given to the Huddersfield Sea Cadets, but *Marsden Shuttle* was busy, being temporarily renamed *Sainsbury's Shuttle* after its sponsors for the Huddersfield Festival in 1993 when festival chairman Gordon Calverley estimated that there were over 10,000 visitors – a record for the Huddersfield event. The bicentenary of the canal was commemorated by Councillor George Speight cutting a cake at Slaithwaite and daffodils by the door of the Transhipment Warehouse planted by John and Jo Young to produce a display reading '200' in Spring 1994. Sales Officer Gay Quilter listed fifteen main events visited by the sales and promotional caravan that year,

David Sumner and Keith Gibson find time for a quiet pint at the Huddersfield Canal Festival 1993. *(HCS)*

Councillor George Speight cuts the cake to mark the bicentenary of the canal, Slaithwaite, 1994. *(HCS)*

from the IWA National Rally at Waltham Abbey on the River Lee and the Black Country Boating Festival to local events such as Mossley Carnival and the Tunnel End Summer Fair.

Shortly after English Partnerships came into being in the spring of 1994, more than £2 million of further Derelict Land Grants were approved. That gave a total of £4,378,362 approved, making the canal the biggest Derelict Land Grant scheme in the area and putting us well and truly in the Premier League of canal restoration. In Tameside a contract worth £737,000 was let to Morrison Construction for the important Staley Wharf project and approval in principle was given to rebuild the Hartshead power station infilled section. This would allow for complete navigation between Stalybridge and Uppermill, with only Lock 12W to block the way, as at the other end of this long stretch of canal a grant of £355,000 was approved to rebuild Frenches Bridge in Greenfield, and Manns Wharf bridge was now almost finished.

The HCS Restoration work in Huddersfield was complete and HCS Restoration Director, Diggle volunteer, and early retiree Eric Crosland took on temporary employment to supervise work in Slaithwaite. At Diggle clearance of lock by-washes was helped by the volunteers who had finally finished the top two locks of the flight, dredging work began and the first lock (30W) was soon emptied of rubble. Dredging in Mossley revealed a completely silted-up winding hole at Waggon Road, known as Mossley Docks to locals of a certain age. Work continued below that, but the poor quality of the washwalls meant more rebuilding was more needed than expected. The extra costs were met by an increase in the grant.

The key to attracting grants had been to show the benefits of restoration. But the L&R report was eight years old. Back in 1982 I thought I was missing something by looking only at jobs related to leisure & tourism. L&R had suggested the canal could be a catalyst for economic regeneration. It was now apparent that restoration, or the prospect of restoration, was being followed by investment, development and jobs. A new study was needed to show what had actually happened, and to deduce likely future prospects. In June 1994 David Sumner, Mike Thompson, BW Regional Manager Derek Cochrane and I interviewed consultants. We decided to appoint the internationally known financial consultants Coopers & Lybrand at a cost of £30,000. This was so important, with regeneration the central theme for English Partnerships, that we did not seek financial help from the local authorities – we just got on with it. I have nothing but praise for the professionalism and enthusiasm of the study team, led by Michael Turley, and their ability to winkle out facts that I knew were needed but didn't know how to get.

Tameside Council engineers Peter Rawson (left) and Lee Holland study their plan for Staley Wharf. *(HCS)*

A few months after the previous photograph and taken from a similar location, this wider view shows the new canal channel at Staley Wharf with the new Bayley Street Bridge in the distance. *(HCS)*

The start of work by HCS Restoration at Diggle was marked by Councillor Brian Mather, the Mayor of Oldham, cutting the first sod as flakes of snowdrift float by on 14 December 1993. Representing HCS were (Left to Right) David Finnis, Ken Wright, Alec Ramsden and Jo Young. *(HCS)*

John McLoughlin and Eric Crosland discussing the work as the infill material is excavated at Lock 23E, Slaithwaite. *(HCS)*

Above: The wide area excavated at 'Mossley Docks'. *(HCS)*

Right: John Sidebottom rebuilding the canal washwall between Locks 12W and 13W, Mossley, 1994 *(HCS)*

The new Manns Wharf Bridge, Greenfield. *(HCS)*

On the morning of 11 October 1994 the Mayor of Oldham re-opened Manns Wharf bridge in Greenfield. Then in the afternoon the circus of VIPs moved to Portland Basin Heritage Centre for the launch of Coopers & Lybrand's report. The cost of restoration to the end of 1993 had been £7,225,000 in local authority-led work and £3,538,854 in HCS-led work. The benefits from this investment were truly astounding, including £51.8 million in private sector development, the creation of 739 jobs and 223 new dwellings. Developments in the canal corridor carried out since work began on the canal had been identified and the developers interviewed (carefully so as not to reveal that the client was HCS). Only a minority of developments were totally dependant on the canal, but Coopers & Lybrand found that the decision to develop had been influenced to a greater or lesser degree by restoration of the canal in almost every case. The canal was indeed acting as a 'catalyst' for investment. They used economic techniques weighting each scheme according to its dependency on the canal to arrive at the benefits that had accrued. They then took what was in effect a snapshot of owners or developers intentions at the time of the study for new development sites identified by the local authorities and local estate agents. The owners or potential developers were again interviewed to establish their intentions and the extent those would be influenced by restoration of the canal. Coopers & Lybrand believed that the future impact of restoration would be private sector investment of £83 million resulting in as many as 2,567 more jobs and creating 614 new dwellings.

The figures were much higher than any of us had expected – but they had a basis of fact. The technique used, which was much more complex than my simplification suggests, raised questions of belief. Would restoration of the canal really create 3,206 jobs? The conclusions were optimistic, but it would be a very brave (or foolhardy) person to say that Coopers & Lybrand were wrong. The main question was – would it convince English Partnerships?

12 It Could be You

The Coopers & Lybrand study immediately repaid its costs many times over. Early in 1995 English Partnerships approved a series of grants to complete restoration of the canal in Tameside apart from Stalybridge.

The narrow channel dredged from Ashton to Stalybridge in 1988 was inadequate. HCS Restoration was contracted to dredge here again. English Nature required care but accepted the need for a wider and deeper channel. The new dredging fleet, repainted blue with prominent HCS logos, was soon on site. Then we were to rebuild Lock 8W, dredge the canal and repair the washwalls between Stalybridge and Scout Tunnel after Morrison Construction had completed a £1.2 million contract to build a new channel through the infilled section here at the old power station site, and a humped bridge at Grove Road to replace the low bridge. Tameside Council was awarded a grant to buy the disused railway embankment between Scout Tunnel and Lock 12W, to remove the embankment and regrade the land. Water seepage had caused the weight of the embankment to push the towpath sideways, distorting the alignment and reducing the canal to a narrow channel below the lock. When the embankment was removed HCS Restoration would repair the damage and restore the lock.

Applications submitted for grant-aid to repair Standedge Tunnel were a step too far. Oldham Council established that English Partnerships may find some of the cost if we could find another funding partner, but an application for matching European money submitted by HCS would take up most of the regional tourism budget. The combination of Derelict Land Grant and European money would not complete restoration of the canal. But there was a new source of possible finance – the National Lottery. In the first few months of the Lottery the draw was peripatetic around the country. HCS was selected as the featured charity when the draw was held at the University of Huddersfield's St Paul's Hall. David Sumner pressed the button to start the draw and was presented with an 'I started the ball rolling' trophy. Sold with the slogan 'It could be you', the National Lottery was a potentially significant funder of waterway restoration. Millions would be raised by the sale of tickets every week. Discussions

The Lottery Draw, January 1995. Left to Right: *Last of the Summer Wine* actress Kathy Staff, David Sumner, and television presenters Gordon Kennedy and Anthea Turner. *(HCS)*

with the local authorities and BW were held in the HCS office in February 1995. From the various lottery boards who were distributing the funds, Sports Council funding might be possible with some imagination, but was not likely to amount to much. The Heritage Lottery Fund was the obvious source, but it would be hard to make a case for the new canal through Stalybridge, Slaithwaite, Sellers and Bates's. It was decided to bid for complete restoration of the canal to the Millennium Commission, who were to fund one-off projects to mark the millennium as the 1990s passed into the 2000s.

Tameside Council wanted to extend the bid to other projects in Stalybridge, including an extension of the Art Gallery, the renovation of the Market Hall and the creation of a waterfront piazza to the river frontage. No imaginative argument could make these relevant to the canal, so two applications would have to be submitted. Tameside Council's application, 'The Stalybridge Millennium Initiative', included the canal through Stalybridge. The second application, for the remainder of the canal, was put together in the HCS office by Steve Whitby and Bob Gough with a lot of help from Mike Thompson and, especially, the local authority planners. Submitted in the Society's name, the details were taken from the bid for resources made to English Partnerships. We knew there was an even larger waterway application to restore the Forth & Clyde and Union Canals in Scotland. Thankfully we would not be in direct competition with that, but the Rochdale Canal Trust had also submitted an application.

On St George's Day, Sunday 23 April 1995, the new canal at Staley Wharf was officially opened by Tom Pendry, MP for Stalybridge and Hyde, at the helm of a 1911 Windermere Launch brought in especially for the day by HCS member Robin Witter. Entertainment was provided with a brass band, a jazz band, morris dancers and circus performers.

Morrison Construction built a new channel through the power station site – directly under a pylon – remarkably quickly. The embankment at Lock 12W was removed and the area landscaped, but the land had to settle before we could rebuild the canal. HCS Restoration had

John Maynard, David Sumner and Bob Dewey received long service awards at the HCS 21st Birthday celebrations, Church Inn, Uppermill, 1995. *(HCS)*

The new channel underneath the pylon alongside the site of the demolished Hartshead Power Station. *(HCS)*

completed dredging, rebuilt wash-walls and restored the towpath all the way from here through Mossley. Further up the valley, local contractor Casey's began work in September to build a new bridge at Frenches in Greenfield. HCS Restoration Deputy Chairman Ken Wright was showing his true colours by helping out as a dredger driver between Lock 1W and Staley Wharf. The HCS Restoration team was busy at Diggle too. Locks 30W and 29W were complete and gated by spring 1995. A few months later work was concentrated on the lower part of the flight of locks. Lock 27W was complete and locks 26W and 28W almost ready for gates. Lock 26W presented a new problem – the paddle culverts were completely filled with concrete that had to be laboriously drilled out. To dredge the bottom pound of the flight between Locks 24W and 25W presented a problem. Our dredger *Pollard* could not be used – there was nowhere to crane it in to the canal, and it was working in Stalybridge. Large land-based plant was out of the question because there was no access on the towpath. In the end a small excavator worked in the canalbed moving silt in several operations – very time consuming and costly; but there was no alternative. We had the occasional problem of vandalism on sites but nothing like the problems in this quiet rural location. The paddle gear was dismantled and the gears smashed, costing several thousand pounds to replace. Then, and potentially more serious, a 2ft (600mm) deep trench was dug through the offside wall of the canal at waterlevel and the by-wash to the lock below blocked. Overnight the water level rose to spill through the trench into Shaw's Pallets factory. Foreman Malcolm Braddock reckoned that it would have taken two men at least ninety minutes to dig the trench. Only minor flooding took place, but it could have been much more serious. The motive remained a mystery and the police never found anyone responsible.

After that dispiriting event I was thrilled to be presented with a Civic Trust commendation on behalf of HCS Restoration for our work as builders on the Transhipment Warehouse.

Opposite: HCS Restoration dredger *Pollard* with mud hopper and tug *Ashton* Staley Wharf, Spring 1996. *(HCS)*

Right: Keith Gibson receives the Civic Trust Commendation on behalf of HCS Restoration Ltd for the work at the Transhipment Warehouse from Councillor John Crowther. *(HCS)*

Then in October the architect Russell Earnshaw and I were presented with commendations by James Wines, an American architect, at the University of Huddersfield in the annual Royal Institute of British Architects White Rose Awards for buildings in the region. We were in good company, with other projects receiving commendations including Huddersfield's McAlpine Stadium.

HCS Restoration was still working on the east side of the canal in the summer of 1995. The canal was dredged between locks 23E & 24E and a new retaining wall built to the road below Lock 24E. In Huddersfield the Derelict Land Grant to rebuild the canal through the former Haigh's Mill site was taken up when the mill site was redeveloped as a new Wickes DIY store. Behind the new store, and largely hidden from view, a brand new concrete channel took water right up to Sellers Engineering. While HCS Restoration was working flatout, a sense of disquiet rumbled on in the background into the spring and summer of 1995 after the arguments in HCS Council about the Transhipment Warehouse. HCS Council became worried that their financial control of HCS Restoration was inadequate. The council decided to adopt new procedures to control expenditure. The principle was unarguable but the detail meant that for even minor expenditure HCS Restoration would have to go cap in hand to the Society Council. The Board of HCS Restoration would not stomach that. I was in the middle of this and had to stand against the proposed changes with increasingly fruitless and bitter arguments. Eventually, of course, the whole thing blew over and relations improved, but trust between council members took time to recover. I rather lost the plot and spent too much time distracted from the crucial process of bidding for grants. Mike Thomson stopped attending council meetings and Gordon Calverley, who had run two superb Huddersfield Festivals, resigned from the council.

Then we received the news that both Tameside Council's and the Society's bids to the Millennium Commission had failed. But the very similar bid for the Rochdale Canal was shortlisted for approval. There were stories in Stalybridge that the HCS bid had scuppered the

The new canal channel to the rear of the Wickes DIY store, Huddersfield. *(HCS)*

Tameside bid, which was obvious nonsense. Luckily neither the Society or the council were fazed by these as we could easily have been side-tracked into a full scale row orchestrated by uninformed opinions.

A funding strategy workshop between BW, HCS and the local authorities, with Mike Turley and Hilary Bell from Coopers & Lybrands to advise, was held at the Transhipment Warehouse in May 1995. David Sumner, Derek Cochrane and Steve Whitby visited the Millennium Commission in London to discuss the possibility of a re-application. David Sumner, Steve Whitby, Mike Thompson, Bob Gough, Ken Wright and I were now very clear about the roles we had to play. Ken Wright chaired meetings with the local authority engineers to ensure we had realistic designs and costs. Bob Gough began looking at ecological issues. And the local authorities and BW began to think again about maintenance. The existing maintenance agreements between the local authorities and BW would not meet the Millennium Commission's requirement of a guaranteed 125 year's maintenance. The tracks between the HCS office and the local authority planning and engineers offices, and with BW at Northwich, were soon taking the strain again as Steve Whitby put together a document that would serve as a basic overview from which a new application could be developed. The total estimated cost increased slightly to £26.5 million, half of which would be sought from the Millennium Commission. HCS would provide £500,000 and British Waterways £400,000. It was decided that the work would be managed by a company limited by guarantee with charitable status whose directors would be appointed by the local authorities, HCS and BW. At the same time Steve Whitby, Mike Thompson and Bob Gough put together a Strategic Programme of Reclamation in October 1995 which combined the inputs of all of the partners to bring the bid to English Partnerships up to date.

To avoid any delay while the local authorities and BW sorted out budgetary issues in paying their share, HCS appointed three consultants chosen to help. PIEDA, planning and economic consultants, would prepare the bid documents; Market Access, lobbying consultants, would ensure that the right people knew of the application and its benefits, and DTW were public relations consultants. The HCS team was expanded to include Alec Ramsden because of his press and PR background and Tameside Council brought in Roger Anderson, the council's Assistant Chief Executive, to lead the project teams developing the application. He soon chaired the first of many meetings at the HCS office with Marion Chalmers of PIEDA, Alex Challoner of Market Access and Robin Treacher of DTW plus the usual suspects from HCS and the local authorities. If the scheme was shortlisted by the Millennium Commission PIEDA would prepare a Business Plan and Market Access would provide lobbying support. The Standedge Experience would be a central feature of the bid. HCS would be the official 'lead partner' with the application submitted in the Society's name. The bid would be put together in the HCS office with number crunching on our computers, but Tameside Council would ease the load by charging planner Steve Hughes with the responsibility for drafting the words of the initial document. Steve Whitby and Bob Gough collated information and presented it in a comprehensive and professional manner. The section covering the Standedge Experience was completed by Mike Thompson and Steve working now with Roger Beckett (the architect of the Canal Museum in Gloucester) and Neil Morton (of Wilde & Partners, HCS's long-standing Consulting Engineers), to develop the concept and produce a draft business plan. Ken Wright was co-ordinating the work of the engineers and I was overseeing both a report by the Civic Trust and Adrian Caley, a local architect/planner. That would provide a heritage and environmental audit of the canal and its surroundings – background information for the Millennium application, but vital if the Millennium bid failed and we had to apply to the Heritage Lottery Fund. *Pennine Link* commented that a great deal of the Society's money was being spent preparing for what we hoped would be a successful bid. But as most of the workload of HCS Restoration was now grant-aided the Society's reserves built up again to £961,660 at the end of 1995.

The application to the Millennium Commission was ceremonially posted at Staley Wharf by Councillors Alan Whitehead, Ken Sims and Alan Griffiths, the Mayors of Tameside, Kirklees and Oldham. The Post Office provided a portable pillar box for press photographs. Looking solid and heavy, if suspiciously ornate, it was plastic, in three sections and transported in Frank Smith's car. The local authority officers intended to feed their civic leaders at the *Wharf* pub but it was being redecorated. Frank Smith came to the rescue with fish and chips from a nearby chippy.

David Sumner took Steve Whitby and Roger Anderson with him when he was asked to speak at a meeting of the Parliamentary Waterways Group on sources of funding. He was somewhat unnerved to sit between Jennifer Page, Chief Executive of the Millennium Commission, and Richard Bradley of English Partnerships. Perhaps that was a good omen. A few days later we received a letter dated 24 April 1996 from Jennifer Page telling us that our application had been selected to go forward for detailed appraisal. And on 16 May Martin Reynolds, Senior Development Manager, English Partnerships, wrote saying that the Strategic Programme of Reclamation had an 'indicative resource allocation' of up to £12 million.

Both organisations sent a checklist of information required. Some items were straightforward; others needed complex negotiations. The work of the consultants began in earnest. The bidding team led by Roger Anderson had several key tasks before passing material to PIEDA for inclusion in the crucial Business Plan. The management arrangement between BW, the local authorities and HCS to guarantee delivery of the project had to be negotiated, as had an arrangement that would guarantee maintenance for the 125 years required by the Millennium Commission. The costs had to be checked again and again and the bidding team had to be certain that there were answers to every question asked. A huge stack of material was turned by PIEDA into a Business Plan to submit to the Millennium Commission and English Partnerships. Market Access ensured that Millennium Commissioners were briefed on the benefits of restoring the canal. After long discussions as to what should be included as a cost and how much of the cost of the bidding process might be reimbursed, the cost of completing restoration of the canal and creating the Standedge Experience was now estimated at around £31 million. HCS would provide £500,000, together with volunteer time valued at £1,185,898, BW would provide £400,000 and the local authorities £710,000. So much work had been done that the partners could say with absolute certainty that the work could be delivered on time and within the estimated cost. That was a clear advantage, as was the evidence of the Coopers & Lybrand report. The local authority planners found some of the development sites identified in that report had already been developed but they could not judge the dependency of this on the canal without further interviews.

The long-standing Joint Committee between the partners, that Trevor Ellis and David Sumner still attended on behalf of HCS, was inadequate for the Millennium Commission; it had no authority to guarantee completion or maintenance. Instead it was proposed that the partners set up a company with directors nominated by BW, the three local authorities and HCS. The company (soon to be registered as the Huddersfield Canal Co.) would appoint a Project Manager. BW and the local authorities, working with the Project Manager, would be responsible to the company for restoring the canal. BW would maintain the canal to cruising standard, but they were only allowed to spend to remainder waterway levels. They produced a schedule listing likely repair and replacement costs for the canal. Maintenance costs would in the first instance be met by the existing BW budget. Costs above that would be met from a Sinking Fund that the local authorities would contribute to for twenty-one years. Because maintenance costs in the early years would be lower than later, the fund would build up to provide capital to pay the extra costs of maintaining a working canal for the 125 years required. Contributions would be divided according to the likely costs in each district with an annual cost of £41,445 to Tameside, £38,325 to Oldham, and £70,280 to Kirklees.

The elements of the programme requiring further development work – Stalybridge and the Standedge Experience – had programmes to bring them to fruition, but there was a remarkable and vital development when Delta Crompton Cables (as Delta Cables had become) closed their factory in Stalybridge. The Millwood Rubber works was already closed. The Chamber of Trade pressed the council to rebuild on the original route through the town rather than canalise the river. Chris Davies, MP for Littleborough and Saddleworth, told the press that the river route would be unlikely to attract grants. Council Leader Roy Oldham would have none of this. He told the *Manchester Evening News* that the council would not listen to people who were 'intent on making decisions with their hearts and not their heads.' A decision would be made when the council had all the facts. The council commissioned engineering consultants Allot & Lomax to carry out a study of the River Tame, and recommend the favoured route. When their report was received, the council very quickly decided, on 27 September 1996, that the canal should be restored along its original route through the town centre. The consultants' report made it clear that now that route was feasible there was actually no choice. The original route would be less expensive, much simpler in operation, and would bring more economic benefits to the town.

Planning permission had been granted to convert the listed warehouse at Tunnel End to the Standedge Experience. The cost of building repairs was known and some idea of the likely cost of providing a visitor centre, but detailed design would only begin after the Canal Company was set up. The Millennium Commission wanted more detail before the application was considered by the Commissioners. HCS could immediately pay consultants, so we appointed Brooke Millar Peden, Architects from Leicester, who were suggested by BW. Within a month they considered the history of Tunnel End and Standedge and the specification, cost and design of a visitor centre. They arranged for another firm of consultants, Archaemedia, to research the history and, setting it in the context of late-eighteenth/early-nineteenth century England, they wrote a fascinating story to form the basis of exhibition material. That was so good that it was serialised in *Pennine Link*. From this Haley Sharpe, designers, developed the design of a visitor centre. But it would cost more than budgeted for. HCS was already committed to £500,000. That figure increased to £550,000 – but we were still short. The Standedge Experience was crucial for Kirklees Council who saw it as vital in the regeneration of the upper Colne Valley. They offered a further £500,000.

By December 1996 HCS and the local authorities had spent £170,000 in staff time and consultants fees on the application. In consultants fees alone the Society had spent nearly

£40,000 plus the £30,000 for the Coopers & Lybrand report two years before. The application was enlarged on, questions answered and gaps filled in by the Business Plan which was delivered to the Commission by PIEDA in time for the Commissioners meeting. Steve Whitby listed everyone involved in *Pennine Link*. I have already mentioned key HCS people, except for John Sully who kept his eye on expenditure and ensured money was available when it was needed. For BW they were Derek Cochrane, Ian Selby, Alex Thomson, Neil Maxwell and Colin Thompson. At the local authorities the three senior planners who had supported us from the early days, Steve Hughes (Tameside), John Miller (Kirklees) and John Billington (Oldham), were helped by engineers Peter Rawson (Tameside), Graham Pointon (Oldham), Shalim (Slim) Chaudary (Kirklees) and landscape architect Geoff Farnell at Kirklees (he had been our prime contact for Derelict Land Grant work) together with planners Nick Andrews and John Rooney from Oldham. Roger Anderson, Tameside's Assistant Chief Executive, oversaw the whole thing. Many hours, way beyond the call of duty, were put in by all of them at the HCS office – and not for the pleasure of Steve Whitby's famous coffeepot.

In November, Government Minister and Millennium Commissioner Virginia Bottomley visited Tunnel End. She told HCS reporter Alec Ramsden that 'water…was of vital importance in the development of the commercial sector and…an agency for regeneration.' There had been constant publicity in the local press about the application and little opposition, although one Slaithwaite resident wrote to the *Huddersfield Examiner* that 'the village has never been as pretty as it is when all the bulbs and trees are in bloom. People of my generation remember the canal with all its rats, dead animals and chip papers.'

Work continued on the canal but at a slowing rate. The dredging between Lock 1W and Staley Wharf was completed in 1996. The HCS workforce had been augmented by part-time dredger/tug drivers (and HCS Restoration directors) Ken Wright, Keith Noble and Eric Crosland. Morrison Construction finished the new canal at the power station site and the bridge at Grove Road. HCS Restoration moved onto the site to rebuild Lock 8W. This was almost a new lock, with sides formed from pre-cast concrete sections faced in engineering brick. Our team had also moved on to Lock 12W after the regraded land had been given time to settle. The lock only needed minor rebuilding but the canal from the lock to Scout Tunnel had not just been distorted by the land slippage, it had experienced 'heave' – physically raising the bed. The complete stretch had to be excavated and rebuilt. The vegetation included plants, which gave the canal its SSSI status, which were carefully transplanted to an offside location above the lock. When the dredging team finished at Staley Wharf, the dredger *Pollard*, tug *Ashton* and the mud hoppers moved on to dredge the canal between Mottram Road through the new channel at Hartshead to Scout Tunnel. English Nature agreed that in some areas only a centre channel would be dredged and in others a shoulder of marginal vegetation would be left. Before work began Freshwater Sponges were relocated to safe water. The Diggle Flight of locks was complete and officially opened on 29 March 1996 by the Mayor of Oldham, Councillor Joe Farquhar. The collapsed wall had been rebuilt at Lock 24E and the guillotine gate fitted, but getting it to work was tricky. The specification agreed with BW required the gate to be galvanised. That caused the large steel gate to twist slightly, which made it stick in the guides. It was intended to plane the timber rubbing strips to achieve a watertight fit, but the Ekke timber specified was very hard and difficult to plane, and the gate was a very tight fit. Below this, Lock 23E adjacent to the infilled length in Slaithwaite was now complete, with attractive hard landscaping and gates. HCS Restoration had rebuilt both walls of the lock chamber. By the end of 1996 HCS Restoration was working on only two sites. Only nine staff remained. The last Community Action Programme trainees had left the workforce. HCS Restoration, and its predecessors, had through various job creation and training programmes found work for around 1,800 trainees and participants since 1984. Most of the tasks remaining would require large contractors, but there was still unfinished work that we were contracted to do, and we were determined to keep a team together in case the Millennium application failed, and to show loyalty to our staff.

HCS Restoration built an almost new lock from reinforced concrete panels that were faced in brickwork at Lock 8W. *(HCS)*

Trevor Wilkinson and Peter Knight concreting the cill in place, Lock 8W. *(HCS)*

The distorted channel between Lock 12W and Scout Tunnel, Mossley. *(HCS)*

Rebuilding the washwall between Lock 12W and Scout Tunnel with stone-faced reinforced concrete units. *(HCS)*

Left: HCS presented plaques to boaters who provided evidence of having made the journey from Ashton to Staley Wharf. Ken Wright submitted this photograph of himself with his application for a plaque, with tug *Ashton* and dredger *Pollard* craned out of the water at Staley Wharf. *(HCS)*

Below: Scout Tunnel the canal was too overgrown to be dredged by *Pollard*. Heavy plant was hired for the occasion. *(HCS)*

There had been the normal quota of Canal Festivals. Luckily the Huddersfield Festival was chaired by the always calm John Leslie in 1995. His mental list of things that might go wrong did not include the wrong marquees being delivered and having to invent a completely new plan of exhibitors and traders on the spot as they arrived. An extra festival was held in May that year, and on several other years during the 1990s, at Uppermill, but the town centre site was small and separated from the canal by the river. Chairman Steve Quilter found that a smaller event hardly reduced the number of volunteers needed. They were difficult to come by for a third event. Even more volunteers were needed in 1995 because the IWA National Trail Boat rally was held over the Easter Bank Holiday weekend between Locks 17E and 19E at Low Westwood, Linthwaite. Twenty-one boats were craned into the water and passed through several locks – the first boats to use them. Visitors came in caravans and tents. The Festival was the usual mixture of trade and craft stalls, canal society stalls, funfair and food trailers with entertainment on the Saturday and Sunday nights. It had been hurriedly arranged by a small HCS group chaired by Alwyn Ogborn after the original location on another canal fell through. Publicity was late and too late for *Pennine Link*. It rained all weekend and, with Huddersfield Town playing at Wembley, local paying visitors were in short supply. Alwyn perhaps found solace when, as editor of *Pennine Link*, he again in 1995 won the IWA award for the best periodical produced by a voluntary waterway organisation. That, however, was his swan song. Work commitments meant spending more time away from home. Ken Wright took over the editor's eyeshade.

On Saturday 11 May 1996 a large number of Society members, friends and guests gathered at Tunnel End to watch Bill Owen launch new larger Marsden trip boats, a tug and butty known jointly as *Standedge Pioneer*. Bill and David Sumner drank a toast and poured champagne over the bows. *Standedge Pioneer* had cost £54,000 and was built by Sagar Marine in Brighouse. Mike Thompson negotiated a grant from the Rural Development Commission and £10,000 came from a secret benefactor. The unique combination for a trip boat of a tug and butty was specially designed by Roger Lorenz to operate on the summit pound where winding holes did not exist. The butty held fifty passengers and was equipped with a lift to provide wheelchair access. The tug powered by a Perkins diesel engine was quite nippy. Most

Andy Sharp carefully brushes a dry mix of sand and cement between the stone setts at Lock 23E, Slaithwaite, 1996. *(HCS)*

Standedge Pioneer – a tug and butty combination – en route from the boatbuilders at Brighouse to Aspley Basin, Huddersfield, from where they were carried by road to Tunnel End, Marsden. *(HCS)*

of the seats on the butty were sponsored by Society members. The sponsors were the first to sail on the new boat with Bill Owen, who made a new fan by sharing his pork pie with my young son Jonathan.

The boat crews shuttled back and forth to Tunnel End through the summer and autumn of 1996 and gave weekend trips from Portland Basin with *Greater Manchester*. Over the Easter break they had provided return trips to Staley Wharf – too long for normal trips but a popular one-off event. Numerous private boats followed *Greater Manchester* up to Staley Wharf to receive a plaque on receipt of proof of passage – a photo, or a 'chitty' from the Wharf Tavern. Apart from weekend boat trips in the pre-Christmas period, the Society was quiet when on 13 December 1996, Jennifer Page, Chief Executive of the Millennium Commission wrote:

> *I am delighted to inform you that the Commission has approved in principle a grant of up to £14,851,241 towards the Huddersfield Narrow Canal project, subject to satisfactory conclusion of negotiations on terms and conditions....*

Pennine Link, delayed to await the news, was issued with a supplement headed 'Santa Says Yes!'

13 The Dream Fulfilled

The offer of the grant meant that the canal should open in the spring of 2000, but it would not be easy to meet the requirements of the Millennium Commission and there was no formal confirmation of the English Partnerships grant.

The Board of the new Huddersfield Canal Co. first met in May 1997. It was agreed that the Chair should rotate annually between each of the partners in turn. Kirklees Councillor George Speight, a long-time supporter of the canal and friend of the Society, was appointed the first chairman. David Sumner and I represented HCS. Alan Stopher, an engineer appointed as project director, took up his appointment on 1 July, at first in a temporary Tameside Council office, but soon moving to the HCS office. The position of HCS within the partnership changed. We had no voting rights in the Joint Committee, but had been the driving force. Now we had equal representation, but our role was diminished. After many years acting as unpaid press officer to the Joint Committee, HCS press officer Alec Ramsden anticipated continuing in that role for the Canal Company, but the local authorities and BW wanted control; their press officers would act for the company. Ken Wright had chaired the regular engineers meetings. These were merged into the officers executive group. Alan Stopher chaired that. David Sumner, Mike Thompson and I had been leaders of the bidding process; now David and I were two members of a Board of Directors. This might have been hard personally but an official 'take-over' of the project was inevitable. Alan Stopher took over from my regular column in *Pennine Link* providing articles on progress.

It took almost a year but, on 28 October 1997, the agreement between the Canal Company and the Millennium Commission was complete and attention could turn to meeting the requirements of English Partnerships. The English Partnerships appraisal would be lengthy and difficult. The Millennium Commission agreed to postpone opening until 2001. Schemes were shown to the public. Wool Road and High Street bridges were presented in an exhibition at Saddleworth Museum. Kirklees displayed an exhibition in a converted Leyland National bus in Slaithwaite, and received a surprisingly favourable reception. Terms were agreed for the acquisition of land for the canal through Stalybridge and at Sellers and Bates's in Huddersfield. Proposals for the Delta Crompton site materialised in the form of a Tesco supermarket alongside the new canal.

BW began preparations for the Standedge Experience by appointing more consultants, Sykes Leisure. They recommended that the cottages should be converted to a licensed café. The canal warehouse would be the visitor centre with the canal arm into the building opened up as the starting point for tunnel trips. I thought this expensive with staff costs difficult to recoup and demanding more volunteers than HCS could provide. I doubted that it would cover its costs, especially as the carpark would be in Marsden ten minutes walk away, and the number of visitors needed to breakeven would remove any sense of tranquillity. BW's Project Manager, Tom Rowe, had second thoughts, suggesting that the warehouse be converted with a free exhibition on the ground floor. The canal arm would still be opened out as the starting point for the tunnel trip and the first floor would have an exhibition that could be visited by those who had bought a ticket for the trip. The second floor would be used as offices by BW. This required less staff and the ground floor exhibition and shop area would be free. The

The official announcement of the Millennium Award at Staley Wharf. Left to Right: Councillor John Battye (Leader, Oldham Council), Councillor George Speight (Kirklees Council), David Sumner (Chairman, HCS), Councillor Michael Ballagher (Mayor, Tameside), Councillor Roy Oldham (Leader, Tameside Council) and Michael Lorkins (Millennium Commission). (Ken Wright)

ground floor of the centre, the tunnel trip and the cottages, which would be let as a licensed café, could be developed, but there was no money for the upper floors.

More and more details were required by English Partnerships. Their consultants, KPMG – taking a pessimistic view for a funding body – naturally disagreed with the figures that Coopers & Lybrand (now PriceWaterhouseCoopers), taking an optimistic view for the bidders, had produced. KPMG said that completion of the canal would create a further 398 jobs, a small amount of commercial floorspace and 106 new dwellings. Hugely different to Cooper's predictions back in 1994 and, I thought, far too conservative to be realistic. Anyway, whatever the truth, KPMG were satisfied. English Partnerships and their government masters decided that the grant would be value for money. On 23 December 1998, almost two years to the day after the announcement of the Millennium Commission grant, English Partnerships also said 'Yes'. A crowd gathered to mark the announcement at Uppermill on 27 January 1999, with Society members dressed in traditional canal costume and songs from Mikron Theatre. The canal ducks were so impressed that their quacking cut off Jim Gill, Regional Director of English Partnerships, in mid-speech. Having delayed *Pennine Link* for the announcement, editor Ken Wright also had the pleasure of announcing that the magazine had again won the IWA Tom Rolt Award.

English Partnerships required a guarantee that the restored canal would be delivered for the approved grant whatever the actual cost. Dave Fletcher, the chief executive of BW, bravely announced that they would underwrite the project, and the local authorities shared the load by entering into similar agreements for the highway bridges. The only unresolved issue was the problem of VAT. With work on the canal carried out by the local authorities or by HCS, we had been able to claim the tax back. BW would be in a similar position, but the partners legal and financial advisors could find no way that the Canal Company could reclaim the tax. That would add around £5 million to the cost. It was, therefore, agreed that BW would receive the grant funds rather than the Canal Company. That transformed everything; the Canal Company would approve and monitor but, with the need to get contractors on site and work finished to an almost impossible timetable, BW took control.

At last the legal agreements between the partners and with the Millennium Commission and English Partnerships could be signed. They included Principal and Supplemental Agreements with the Millennium Commission, Deeds of Dedication and Certificates of Title to land, an Operation and Maintenance Agreement with the Millennium Commission, Gap Funding and Expenditure Agreements with English Partnerships, a Memorandum of Understanding between the Huddersfield Canal Co. and each of the partners and individual agreements between British Waterways and the local authorities for each contract to be let on the canal. It was all a bit much to understand – especially as everything had to be rewritten at the last minute to reflect the fact that BW would act as banker. And it was nearly too much to achieve. The agreement between BW and English Partnerships was not signed and exchanged until 5.30 p.m. on 31 March 1999 – just in time, as the government passed the grant-giving responsibilities of English Partnerships to new Regional Development Agencies on the following day.

HCS had continued as normal throughout the long wait. The boat crews were busy. *Greater Manchester* gave trips on the Peak Forest Canal to Hyde from Portland Basin and *Oldham Otter* (as *Marsden Shuttle* had been renamed when *Standedge Pioneer* was delivered) gave short trips from Audenshaw on the Ashton Canal. But *Standedge Pioneer* was out of service by the end of 1998 with de-watering of the canal expected to allow work to begin in the tunnel. It was so wet at the Uppermill Festival in 1997 that the dog show judge had to be carried across the field. The Tameside Festival that year was drier, but Chairman Peter Hawley had problems with the craft tent. An agent commissioned to arrange traders ceased trading, then, after hurriedly finding traders, the generator providing electricity to the stalls was stolen in the middle of the night. Perhaps the best thing was the Staley Wharf Rally of Boats organised by Alwyn Ogborn. After practising with the IWA Trail Boat Rally, he knew something about boat rallies and this event was arranged for the May Bank Holiday in 1997. Boats started to arrive at Staley Wharf on the Friday evening but water supply through the Stalybridge culvert was slow. Saturday saw boats grounded, pushed and pulled to get over the mud like the pioneering days when rallies were held on impossible navigations. By persistence and determination twenty-five boats made it to the site.

On 15 April 1998 I was invited to take a few turns with a lock key to officially commission the new guillotine gate at Lock 24E at Slaithwaite with Dennis McInnes, English Partnerships' Yorkshire Regional Senior Development Manager. We cut a ceremonial ribbon and thanked all those involved. This would be the last restoration work on the canal by HCS; from now on it would be up to the partnership, the Huddersfield Canal Co. and BW.

With a weekly wage bill of £3,500 the future of HCS Restoration was a worry. HCS was dependent on the staff and the Mossley Road base, but work on the canal was almost at a standstill in 1997. The only work taking place was between Lock 12W and Scout Tunnel, where the canal was rebuilt using pre-cast concrete abutments to form the nearside wall while the offside washwall was repaired. After that we only had work to complete from earlier grant approvals – dredging between Grove Road and Lock 9W and the dredging and repair of washwalls between Lock 11W and Scout Tunnel. Steve Whitby tried to find general building work but could not compete with small contractors working from home. The much-reduced HCS Restoration workforce continued into 1998 but the prospect of further work was bleak. BW suggested they might take on the employment of our outdoor staff, but they could not take the managerial and office staff. In the event more repairs were needed between Scout Tunnel and Grove Road than anticipated which kept our workforce busy for a few months, and we expected to be offered a contract to repair Dungebooth and Lime Kiln locks, the first contract of the Millennium project. These were the locks in Uppermill where volunteers started restoration. The volunteers had cleared out and re-gated the locks, but nearly twenty

Dennis McInnes (English Partnerships Yorkshire Region) looks on while Keith Gibson raises the guillotine gate at Lock 24E. *(HCS)*

HCS Restoration fitting lockgates, Dungebooth Lock, March 1999. *(HCS)*

years later there were signs of movement to the walls. If we could continue with small jobs or sub-contract work until restoration was almost complete, new jobs needed to maintain the canal and at the Standedge Experience might give our staff the chance of continued employment. Then BW decided to increase their maintenance staff sooner rather than later; they wanted people in post well before re-opening so that they did not have inexperienced staff on the opening day.

Alan Stopher persuaded the Millennium Commission that the Uppermill locks work could begin before the release of the main funding if the partners footed the bill. Grant aid would be paid retrospectively. HCS agreed to make available up to £300,000 from our commitment to the Standedge Experience, and the contract was let to HCS Restoration. It involved dredging between Wade Lock and Wool Road and repairs to the two locks. Work started in November 1998 and new lock gates were ordered this time all the way from Holland. As HCS Restoration neared the end of the Uppermill work and the dredging and washwall repair below Scout Tunnel was completed, work was rapidly running out when Steve Whitby found extra work under contract to Tameside Council to restore the infilled Alma Street Arm of the Peak Forest Canal near Portland Basin. This involved digging out the canal, rebuilding wash walls, reconstructing the entrance to the Ashton Canal, restoring a brick footbridge, towpath work and landscaping. The restored site was to be developed as a boatyard bringing to fruition a long held dream of the developer, Guy Holding.

After this the work available was very limited and that would be by competitive tender. HCS Restoration was no longer the 'cheap' option it had been when we were working on two or three large contracts supported by job creation or training labour. The company was too small to compete for the large contracts, but it was too big to compete for smaller contracts or sub-contract work. It had costs that would not be carried by potential competitors – a larger office/workshop than required for the reduced scale of operation, plant and vehicles that competitors would hire in, and a permanent workforce with a range of abilities with paid holidays and sickness entitlement. Likely competitors would set on and lay off staff as needed and subcontract out skilled work. HCS could pay the office staff who were needed to support the Society and the Canal Company directly, but costs would still be too high to compete. To be competitive we would have to reduce costs dramatically, make staff redundant and employ

The last project for HCS Restoration. The re-opened Alma Street arm of the Peak Forest Canal, Ashton-under-Lyne. *(HCS)*

labour only as and when required, and with very different terms of employment. There would be considerable risks and no guarantee of employment for staff. On 5 May 1999 a joint meeting of the Board of Directors of HCS Restoration and HCS Council decided to close down HCS Restoration when current contracts were completed. Frank Ruffley, the original Chairman of the Company, moved the motion. I seconded it. Staff would be made redundant on 31 August. Steve Whitby would stay to wind-up the operation.

It was a sad decision and ironic that our staff, many of whom had been involved in restoration of the canal for many years, should have to go just as we were on the final straight. Naturally people looked for scapegoats. BW was the prime candidate. The truth of the matter was that time and events dictated the situation. BW had considered taking on some of our staff, but at a time when we had contracts to fulfil. They had then expanded their own maintenance force on the canal. That was needed, but, realistically, any hope of finding a simple end to HCS Restoration and continuing work for our staff was then beyond redemption. HCS had been unusual amongst waterway restoration societies in employing staff and unique in having a subsidiary contracting business. The company had restored twenty-five locks, with two more underway at Uppermill (so the Society, including volunteers, would ultimately have restored twenty-nine locks), dredged about six miles of canal, rebuilt washwalls, repaired eleven miles of towpath (five on the Peak Forest), carried out the award-winning restoration of the Transhipment Warehouse and environmental and landscaping works. Steve Whitby had been intimately involved in bidding for funds, and, together with Mike Thompson and Bob Gough he had brought together the work from the other partners to produce the original programme for the Millennium Commission and English Partnerships grant applications. Final staff were: Steve Whitby, Managing Director; John McLoughlin, General Manager; Bob Gough, OM Technical Section (OM meaning 'One Man'!); Paula McLoughlin, Admin Officer; Andy Sharp, General Foreman; Chris Sharp, Craftsperson; Ken Williams, Craftsperson; Roy Williams, Craftsperson; Trevor Wilkinson, Labourer and James Wood, Labourer. Society notables Ken Wright, Keith Noble, Eric Crosland and John Wilson had also been employed on a part-time occasional basis as needed. The thing I found most difficult about this whole situation – and I had always been rather in the background to many of our staff – was that these were my friends who were to be sacked.

Work was completed at Uppermill in early July. Paula McLoughlin found a job with British Airways, Andy Sharp was soon working with a leading masonry firm and Jimmy Wood and Trevor Wilkinson found jobs with BW. Steve Whitby, John McLoughlin and Bob Gough remained to tidy things up. Meanwhile Ken Wright again won the Tom Rolt award for *Pennine Link*, but things were not going smoothly in the office. There was not enough work to keep both Steve Whitby and Frank Smith occupied through the summer off 1999, although there would be a lot to be sorted out to agree final accounts on the last contracts. In September it was decided that Steve should be made redundant. He had been a tower of strength for the Society and it was tragic that this decision had to be taken. Bob Gough remained in the office as assistant editor of *Pennine Link*, helping Frank and providing a back-up service to Alan Stopher. General Manager John McLoughlin, who had been our second employee after Steve, agreed to come in part-time to finalise the accounts of completed work, dispose of the assets and leave appropriate records.

As work started on the main contracts, everything depended on the engineers: Tom Rowe, Mike Marshall and Colin Thompson at BW, Peter Rawson and Lee Holland at Tameside, Mike Thompson (no relation!), Freda Rashdi and Joanna Heap at Oldham, Slim Chaudary and Andy Wheeler at Kirklees, with BW's Philip Wright charged with delivering the visitor centre at Tunnel End and John Hallam with supervising work in Standedge Tunnel. BW was responsible for work on the canal track, but most of the detailed design and supervision involving bridges or municipal works would be done by the engineering departments of the three local authorities. The work would create important precedents for waterway restoration nationally by expanding the scope of work carried out to restore a canal. After Standedge Tunnel was re-opened, no other derelict tunnel could seem so difficult and, after almost a mile of new canal had been built through the centres of Slaithwaite and Stalybridge, no other infilled urban canal could be seen as beyond the realms of possibility.

BW awarded the Standedge Tunnel contract to Amalgamated Construction Ltd. By September 1999, when a visit was arranged for the Canal Company Board, the canal was dammed to provide settlement lagoons and a hardcore access road led into the tunnel at the

Tunnel End, Marsden, December 1999. Silt was pumped from Standedge Tunnel to centrifuges at each end of the tunnel, which separated water from dry waste. The canal was temporarily filled in to create settling tanks. *(Alan Stopher)*

Wool Road, Dobcross, November 1999. Formwork in place for the deck of the new Wool Road bridge, with the Transhipment Warehouse beyond. *(Alan Stopher)*

Diggle end. Silt was mixed with water in the tunnel and pumped through a large centrifuge machine from which emerged reasonably dry solid material and amazingly clear water, which was returned to the canal. At Wool Road contractors, DCT Civil Engineering, had uncovered the old canal bridge intact close to Lock 24E. The infilled canal between the basin and this bridge was re-excavated and construction of the concrete main road bridge had begun. The same contractor had been appointed for High Street bridge. Tameside had let the contract at Stalybridge to Dew Construction. The developer of the supermarket would also employ them for the bridges across the canal to the car park. In Huddersfield Yorkshire Water was constructing a deep sewer diversion required before work could begin at Queen Street South bridge.

HCS Council members walked the canal in September 2000. The transformation was incredible. A new waterfront was developing through Stalybridge and the new Mottram Road bridge was complete. Above this Lock 7W was well advanced using half of the original structure with the remainder built in reinforced concrete. The canal was complete between Mottram Road and Armentières Square. The new Lock 6W had started to rise from a massive excavation in Armentières Square early in the year; it now had gates. The square was being paved with high quality modern materials. Rubble filling the arch of Melbourne Street bridge below the square had been dug out, a new channel built, and attractive stone parapet walls replaced the previous mish-mash of repairs to the bridge. The Castle Hall sports centre had been demolished and the buried Lock 5W unearthed in good condition. It was being repaired. The concrete channel upstream and downstream of the lock was formed, and a new Lock 4W had been built next to the petrol station in Caroline Street.

Pointing and rock bolting was complete at Scout Tunnel and BW had repaired the Royal George Aqueduct between Greenfield and Mossley. At Wool Road the new stone-faced bridge was open. Lock 24W above the bridge, which had been buried, had been excavated, repaired and received its new set of gates with an official opening on 19 May with Millennium

Stalybridge town centre, January 2000. A pre-cast concrete bridge unit is being placed for the service road bridge at Armentières Square. The steel reinforcing for the new Lock 6W is visible beyond. *(Alan Stopher)*

Stalybridge town centre, February 2000. Steel reinforcement and shuttering being prepared for the new concrete channel on the site of the old Lock 6W in what had been the yard area of the former Delta Crompton factory. Building works are also taking place alongside the canal on the site of the new supermarket. *(Alan Stopher)*

Above: Standedge Tunnel. Mesh fixed to rock bolts in a section of bare rock tunnel where the surface was liable to fragment. It will be sprayed with a thin layer of concrete. *(Alan Stopher)*

Opposite: The waterways warehouse at Tunnel End, Marsden scaffolded as work progressed on the creation of the Standedge Visitor Centre. *(Alan Stopher)*

Commissioner Judith Donovan present. The arch of the original High Street bridge had been reconstructed and was carrying traffic as work started on building an extension to the bridge. Wade Lock had been repaired. Old Sag Aqueduct directly above Lime Kiln lock had been strengthened with a concrete saddle installed within the arch.

At Standedge Tunnel a second centrifuge had been used, removing silt at the Marsden end. Rock bolting of lose rock followed; 90% of the rock bolts were installed and sections of bare rock that might flake off were stabilised by a mesh and sprayed concrete lining. Work was continuing on the removal of debris from rock falls and repairs to adits and shaft bases. A new arch at the rock fall near the Marsden end was almost complete.

In Slaithwaite contractors Galliford Northern were working on Britannia Road bridge. Paving was complete along Carr Lane where a temporary oneway system around the village had ended to the relief of the shopkeepers. Above the bridge a retaining wall alongside the river had been strengthened so that a new bridge to the canalside road could be built across the canal below Lock 23E. The old Lock 22E, which was buried in the carpark, had been excavated and practically rebuilt. To avoid damage to canalside building foundations, only a narrow concrete channel had been built from here opposite the village shops to Lock 23E apart from a wider mooring space just above the lock. Downstream a wider channel had been built to the site of the new Lock 21E including a large turning area below Lock 22E. Stone cladding was being fixed to the concrete walls of the channels. The reinforced concrete structure of Lock 21E was being completed beside Platt Lane where traffic was using the new canal bridge. A new car park had been constructed on the site of an old council depot on New Street. David Littlewood of the Colne Valley Trust chaired regular liaison meetings

Building the new concrete channel through Slaithwaite, August 2000. *(Alan Stopher)*

between residents, the business community, council and contractors. In the centre of the village the canalside frontage of Globe Mills had been stone cleaned.

Further down the valley Wrekin Construction had completed new stone-faced bridges at Lees Mill, Holme Mill and Stoney Battery, and repaired the Golcar Aqueduct. BW ecologist Nick Birkenshaw and Huddersfield University students had rescued several hundred white-clawed crayfish and transferred them upstream.

In Huddersfield at Sellers Engineers, contractors Costains had built a car park and access road to release land for the canal. Two rows of sheet piling walls were installed alongside the firm's tin shop, concrete cross member slabs cast over the piles, and the new canal tunnel excavated from within the box so created. Lock 3E was being constructed at the upstream end of the site to join up with the channel behind the Wickes DIY store. The steel frame of a new grinding shed and electrician's shop was being clad with metal panels. When machinery was transferred to this building the old grinding and electricians' shops would be demolished, allowing the tunnel to be extended to the new lock. At the nearby Bates's Mill the teasing shed had been cleared of machinery, a trench dug across the floor and concrete piles driven here on either side of the future canal. The floor of the building had been reinstated and the tunnel excavated by digging between the piles. The breakthrough to Queen Street South bridge, after clearing the course between the piles of the 1980s building, had taken place in July. Work on the sewer diversion under the canal was complete and the listed bridge had been underpinned to allow the canal channel to be deepened. Work was concentrating on construction of the deep steel-piled channel downstream and on a new Lock 2E upstream of Bates's.

The contract for building work at the Standedge Visitor Centre – no longer to be called the Standedge Experience – had been let to Wakefield contractor Lemmeleg. BW engaged Architecture & Design Partnership to lead the design team; they had been the architects for the Transhipment Warehouse and, coincidentally, also for Sellers Engineers' new building.

By Christmas structural repairs to Standedge Tunnel were complete, the work through Slaithwaite and at High Street, Uppermill, was almost finished and water returned to the canal through Stalybridge. A new bridge at Caroline Street linked the new channel to Staley Wharf

Bates & Co., Huddersfield, December 1999. Installing reinforced concrete piles to form the tunnel sides through the floor of the factory building. Bates's sub-contracted out their work that would have taken place in the building and cleared the floor of machinery for the two months that the contractors occupied the building. *(Alan Stopher)*

Constructing the 320m long tunnel at Sellers Engineers, Huddersfield, February 2000. Temporary supports are in place to hold the sheet piled walls apart until the concrete base slab is poured. Pre-cast concrete slabs will be placed to form the roof. *(Alan Stopher)*

Bates & Co., June 2000. The floor of the building has been reinstated, and the 90m-long tunnel is being excavated between the concrete piles. A mini excavator (in the background) is loading spoil onto a skip wagon on a narrow gauge railway. The skip was taken out of the workings and lifted by crane to be emptied in a waiting truck adjacent to the new Lock 2E. *(Alan Stopher)*

and Locks 5W and 7W had gates. The completion of Lees Mill bridge, Holme Mill bridge, Golcar Aqueduct and Stoney Battery bridge was marked by a plaque unveiled by the Mayor of Kirklees, Councillor Ann Denham, and BW Regional Director, Derek Cochrane. In Huddersfield the reinforced concrete structure of Lock 3E was nearing completion. Massive machines were being moved into Sellers' new building to allow the redundant building to be demolished and the final length of tunnel built. At Bates's Mill Lock 2E had received gates, the contractor was preparing the tunnel walls for sealing with sprayed concrete and the deep channel between Queen Street South bridge and the old Lock 2E was nearly complete. And the design for the three battery-powered Standedge Tunnel tug boats and towed passenger modules (as the passenger carrying butties are called – one for the tunnel trip, and one to carry boat crews) was being finalised by BW.

The voluntary sector contribution to funding, as submitted in the application to the Millennium Commission, became unacceptable as work progressed. The Commission decided that they would only accept the value of volunteers' contributions to restoration, which would not include the value of running boats or festivals. That would reduce their grant by about £500,000, which could have been critical. BW came to the rescue, and also to the rescue of the Standedge Visitor Centre. There was insufficient money for the upper floors or even to provide a staircase. The limitations of spending on a remainder waterway did not apply to their property portfolio, so BW decided to invest £490,000 of their own money. That neatly solved two problems; it allowed for the complete Visitor Centre and gave sufficient matching funding for the complete Millennium Commission grant to be received. Work was well under way on re-roofing of the warehouse in early 2001 and Headland Design Associates was engaged to design and construct the exhibits.

The rush to complete the Visitor Centre, with work extended to the upper floors, meant that BW-appointed architects, design consultants and a centre manager with no consultation with the Society or Kirklees, who were both making large financial contributions. Philip Wright who was in charge of completing the physical work, buckled down to the task and delivered this large and complex project in an incredibly short time. When HCS Council considered the visitor centre Joint Venture Agreement between the Society, Kirklees and BW, the idea of refusing to sign up in disapproval at the lack of consultation, and what I saw as the centre's resulting shortcomings, was appealing, but too much was at stake. When the official handing over of the Society's cheque took place, Treasurer John Sully was delayed on a train. I dutifully deputised by handing over a large facsimile of the cheque for the benefit of the press.

Suddenly, we had an almost complete canal. The programme at Sellers and Bates's was tight right from the start and, although work was on schedule, the canal would not be ready until a day or two before the end of April 2001, but the west side was finished and BW decided to 'unlock' the canal to Dobcross. So on 9 April we celebrated by bringing three small boats, *Astra* which we were hiring for the year to accompany *Marsden Shuttle* (which after repainting was given back its old name), *Magic Maker* and *Little Gypsy*, through Stalybridge. *Forget-me-not* a traditional wooden boat followed with a cargo of timber for the Wooden Canal Boat Society's new boatyard in Stalybridge.

After the wettest winter on record and a cold wet spring, the day when all the canal would be open, 1 May, was totally unexpected – a glorious spring day. Although the canal had been open to Wool Road for three weeks, there had been little publicity and only a few boats ventured on to the canal. Even the press calls for the opening day celebrations organised by Tameside and Kirklees Councils were low-key. The last thing wanted was a massive influx of boaters that neither the canal or BW staff were ready for. Only two of the three tunnel tugs had been delivered – and those still in primer. The passenger module boats for the tunnel trip, and to carry the crews of boats being towed through Standedge, had not arrived. For the first few weeks trips into the tunnel would be made courtesy of *Standedge Pioneer*, pushed or towed by the electric tug, and boat crews would be taken over the top by minibus. And there had been no time to practice towing convoys of boats.

The canal between Armentières Square and the new supermarket, Stalybridge, finished but not yet open, waiting for boats. *(Alan Stopher)*

At Portland Basin there were speeches from the assembled dignitaries. Councillor Roy Oldham, Leader of Tameside Council, praised the Council's engineer Peter Rawson and the vision, tenacity and patience of HCS. At Armentières Square the VIP party boarded *Pennine Moonraker* brought down from Uppermill. The delight of John Lund and his crew on being unfettered from the short Uppermill length was apparent. Bob Dewey and Derek Walker, now Chairman of the Derby & Sandiacre Canal Society, were in the crowd. Derek was wearing an original HCS t-shirt overprinted with the dates 1974 and 2001. Eventually *Pennine Moonraker* set off up the canal to accompanying cheers and applause. Then in Huddersfield a little convoy of three boats led by *Ogley*, the mayor's 45ft (13.7m) narrow boat was waiting above Lock 1E to go through the Bates's and Sellers' tunnels. Below the lock, boaters waiting to come through included HCS Council member Keith Noble (who would make the second east-west passage) and Society Treasurer John Sully who was running around like a kid with a new toy. After more words for the press the Mayor set off and, standing at the front of the boat, cut the tape. There was a slight hiatus as the second boat collected a tarpaulin around its propeller, but it was soon cleared, and all three boats were through the tunnels and the new locks. I was on *Savile*, the Calder Navigation Society trip boat, standing by Mr Bates and his son. Their reaction to navigating the tunnel under their premises, and then under Sellers, was much the same as mine – sheer delight and a sense of wonder. We disembarked above the new Lock 3E to more speeches. It was appropriate that the canal should be opened in the year Ann Denham, a boater, was Mayor. Like Councillor Oldham earlier in the day, she made the point that without the Society the canal would not have been restored. Alan Stopher praised Kirklees engineer Andy Wheeler; the design and construction of these two tunnels in very confined spaces through and under working factories was a magnificent achievement.

In the evening it was the premiere at Huddersfield University, overlooking the canal, of Mikron Theatre Company's show *Warehouse Hill* about the restoration of the canal. I was

Above left: Leicester with John Sully at the new Lock 3E beyond the Sellers' Tunnel. Huddersfield,
1 May 2001. *(Trevor Ellis)*

Above top right: The Mikron Theatre production *Warehouse Hill*, 2001. Left to Right: Tracey Holderness,
Charley Moon and Richard Povall. *(Mikron Theatre Company)*

Above right: Until the new tunnel trip boat was delivered, the passenger butty boat *Standedge Pioneer*
was lent to British Waterways to operate trips into Standedge Tunnel propelled by one of the new battery
powered tunnel tugs. *(HCS)*

anxious about what it might contain – if too many HCS people were recognisable there
would be others who felt left out. I needn't have worried. Only John Maynard and David
Sumner were immediately recognisable – and that was how it should be. HCS had always
been a team effort. And the show was very good.

It was fitting that, when it reached Huddersfield, the first boat from end to end was the
Wooden Canal Boat Society's 150-year-old-horsedrawn boat *Maria*, crewed by HCS member
Sue Day. But there were problems for boaters and criticism of the partnership between BW,
the local authorities and HCS. We should have done more. We should have done better.

Kirklees Mayor, Councillor Ann Denham, cuts the tape in the new deep channel below Bates's Mill to inaugurate navigation through the new Bates's and Sellers' tunnels. *(John Lower)*

Passing boats below Lock 3W, Stalybridge. *(John Lower)*

I found myself asking: 'How?' 'When?' and 'Where was the money to come from?' Restoration of the canal had cost about £45 million – it's difficult to be precise when much of the early work created jobs or provided training and included environmental work. It sounds a lot of money but most of the time there was only just enough. Some of the early work was nearly twenty years earlier. It was not surprising that lockgates leaked and paddle gear was difficult to work or more dredging was needed. With 200 years of ground movements since the canal was built, it was not surprising if some lock chambers were not quite parallel-sided or had high spots on the walls that squeezed any boat an inch or two wider than ideal. Even when locks were rebuilt, the walls had been taken down only until sound material was reached and rebuilt from there. There was never the money to completely rebuild locks. No doubt there were also leaks in the canal, possibly not revealed until water started flowing because of boats moving or the emptying and filling of locks. The tunnel had always been narrow – IWA founders Aickman and Rolt had a fright when they squeezed *Ailsa Craig* through – and modern boats are much squarer in profile than the working boats the canal was built for. None of this was any different from the experience of other restored canals. All had been difficult to work at first. The Kennet & Avon had re-opened in 1990 but it was only ten years later with £25 million of lottery funding that the canal was easy to use. Many of the problems would resolve themselves simply through use – gaps between the timbers of most lockgates would seal as the wood expanded through exposure to water, and paddle gear would become freer-moving with use. Other problems would require work and that would be something that the partnership of BW, HCS and the local authorities would have to tackle. For myself, I was content. We had achieved what the Society had set out to do. The big money was dependent on a partnership and the untiring efforts of the local authorities and BW, but the canal would not have been restored if it had not been for the Society's efforts.

The money had not been found to benefit waterway enthusiasts or boaters, but because of the effect of the restored canal in the valleys. It was early days, but it looked to me as though Coopers & Lybrands could be proved right. There was a new sense of optimism, and people around on a weekend in Stalybridge or Slaithwaite, which had previously been deserted. Record prices were paid for houses – in Stalybridge it was said this was throughout the town, not just by the canal. The warehouse there alongside Mottram Road, that had been empty for years, was being converted to flats with new houses alongside. Armentières Square with its central canal lock had put a new heart into the town. Even the derelict Longlands Mill by Lock 5W was subject to interest by developers. And in the Colne Valley Low Westwood Mill, built immediately after the canal opened in Linthwaite but derelict and roofless for years, was subject to a planning application for conversion to dwellings. Further down the valley Union and Burdett Mills on opposite sides of the canal at Milnsbridge had already been converted to flats with new houses between them and the canal basin in the village.

Then it was time for Oldham Council to share in the celebration with an event at Uppermill on 18 May. The local community was well represented amongst the guests invited by the council. There was an amazingly atmospheric moment when *Pennine Moonraker* emerged from High Street bridge to break a tape across the canal, as a fanfare specially written by composer Derek Broadbent was struck up by Diggle Brass Band. On 25 May the Standedge Visitor Centre was officially opened. After welcoming speeches by Tom Rowe, now promoted to Waterway Manager South Pennine Ring, and Millennium Commissioner Judith Donovan, eighty-six years young Lily Turner unveiled a stone tablet commemorating the event. Her father, David Whitehead, was one of the last people to be employed as an official 'legger' through Standedge Tunnel and is claimed to hold the record – eighty-three minutes from portal to portal in 1914. Then from the bows of the trip boat (which had at last

Standedge Tunnel official opening 25 May 2001. British Waterways Chairman, George Greener ready to cut the tape as Diggle Brass Band prepare to play 'Rule Britannia'. (Alan Stopher)

Lock 6W, the centrepiece of Armentières Square, Stalybridge. The Stalybridge Renaissance Festival, May 2001. *(Alan Stopher)*

been delivered) George Greener, the Chairman of BW, declared Standedge Tunnel open as he cut a tape across the mouth of the tunnel. He was accompanied by Regional Director Derek Cochrane, and long-standing BW employee and friend of HCS Fred Carter, promoted to tunnel guide. Very fittingly Diggle Band played *Rule Britannia*. Local microbrewery, Riverhead, brewed a special beer, Standedge Admiral, named for Thomas Bourne, the tunnel-keeper in the canal's years of prosperity and known as the Standedge Admiral. That weekend was the Spring Bank Holiday and Tameside Council organised a festival in Stalybridge. Brass bands, a funfair, a Victorian street market and street performers enlivened the weekend. A gala dinner was held on the Sunday evening and a ceremony on the Monday afternoon, with new bridges named Oldham's Bridge and Ruffley's Bridge after the leader of the council, Roy Oldham, and Frank Ruffley, now an elder statesman for the canal.

The volunteers who had done so much to make the impossible happen had been rather forgotten in the official celebrations. David Sumner and I, no doubt invited as Directors of the Canal Company, had represented the Society. Ken Wright had been there, as editor of *Pennine Link*, and others had just come along. At last the volunteers were given a chance to shine when HCS held its own celebration at the Standedge Visitor Centre on 21 July. It was an all-day event attended by 280 members, with a barbecue, more of the wonderful Standedge Admiral, Marsden Brass Band, a series of coach trips to show members what had been achieved and trips into the tunnel. David Sumner made a speech, that could be summarised as 'Thank you, you made it possible.'

Finally on Monday 3 September came the official opening by HRH The Prince of Wales. As the Royal Train drew up in Marsden Station a cheering crowd greeted the Prince. They followed him as he walked along the towpath to the Visitor Centre accompanied by Dave Fletcher, the Chief Executive of BW and Derek Cochrane. At Tunnel End they were met by children from CragRats Youth Theatre Group in Victorian costume and a performance from Chol Theatre of Batley – but I didn't see any of that. I was waiting with the official party in

The official opening, 3 September 2001. HRH The Prince of Wales talking to David Finnis watched by (left to right) Keith Gibson, David Fletcher (Chief Executive, British Waterways) and Derek Cochrane (Regional Director, British Waterways). *(David Finnis)*

The official opening, 3 September 2001. HRH The Prince of Wales returning from a trip into Standedge Tunnel with (left to right) Derek Cochrane (Regional Director, British Waterways), David Sumner (Chairman, Huddersfield Canal Society) and David Fletcher (Chief Executive, British Waterways). *(David Finnis)*

At last the people of Marsden can watch boats go by. *(John Lower)*

the Visitor Centre. Here Prince Charles was introduced to groups representing BW, the local authorities, the funding bodies and HCS. Representing HCS were David Sumner, Trevor Ellis, Brian Minor, Jo Young, David Finnis (who had returned to the fold), Frank Smith and myself. The Prince shook hands with us and chatted for a few minutes, showing a genuine appreciation of the role of volunteers in restoring the canal. After a short trip into the tunnel he emerged, with the sun at last peeping through, to unveil a brass waymarker by local artist Lynne Chambers as he formally declared the canal open.

The impossible dream had been realised and had the seal of Royal approval. The end of our story, and the beginning of another in the life of the Huddersfield Narrow Canal; an operational waterway and, again, the centrepiece of two Pennine valleys.

The Canal Restored

Obstructions to navigation are listed with notes on who carried out the work, with dates. The canal pounds between locks are not listed unless infilled or built on. Those that remained in water, many of which were silted up or filled with rubbish, were dredged, canal washwalls and towpaths repaired by Tameside Canals Ltd, HCS Restoration Ltd or Kirklees Council.

ASHTON-UNDER-LYNE

Whitelands Road Bridge:	Concrete dam enclosing sewer immediately below bridge. North West Water Authority. 1988.
Lock 1W Ashton Lock:	Concrete cap. TCL 1987.
Lock 2W:	Cascaded, locktail bridge extended over lock. Bridge: George Dews for Senior Service 1986. Lock: TCL 1986/7.
Lock 3W:	Cascaded. TCL 1985/6.

STALYBRIDGE

Stalybridge Aqueduct:	Intact. Dredged TCL 1986/7.
Stalybridge Town Centre:	Canal filled in and water piped for 1,030m.
Bayley Street Bridge:	Piped culvert, bridge infilled. Morrison Construction for Tameside Council. DLG 1994/5. New bridge.
Canal infilled:	Morrison Construction for Tameside Council. DLG. Staley Wharf project 1994/5.
Caroline Street Bridge:	Piped culvert, bridge removed. Dew Construction. Millennium Project. 1999-2001. New bridge.
Petrol filling station:	Extended over route of canal. Dew Construction. Millennium Project. 1999-2001. Canal realigned around petrol station.
Lock 4W:	Buried part under petrol filling station. Dew Construction. Millennium Project. 1999-2001. New lock on realigned canal.
Castle Hall Sports Centre:	Built partly over route of canal. Dew Construction. Millennium Project. 1999-2001. Sports Centre demolished. New canal channel.
Lock 5W Castle Hall Lock:	Part buried under Sports Centre. Dew Construction. Millennium Project. 1999-2001. Lock unearthed and repaired.
Garage business:	Over route of canal. Dew Construction. Millennium Project. 1999-2001. New canal channel and bridge to Back Melbourne Street.
Melbourne Street Bridge:	Piped culvert, bridge infilled. Dew Construction. Millennium Project. 1999-2001. Bridge repaired. New parapet walls.
Armentières Square:	Car park. Dew Construction. Millennium Project. 1999-2001. New canal channel and public space.
New lock 6W:	Dew Construction. Millennium Project. 1999-2001. New lock in centre of square.
Trinity Street:	Piped culvert, bridge removed. Traffic re-routed around new locktail bridge to Lock 6W.
Delta Cables:	Factory building and yard. Demolished, supermarket erected on site. Dew Construction. Millennium Project. 1999-2001. New canal channel.
Lock 6W:	Buried in factory yard. Replaced by new lock 6W.
Millwood Rubber Co.:	Factory building and yard. Dew Construction. Millennium Project. 1999-2001. Canal unearthed, repaired and relined.
Mottram Road Bridge:	Piped culvert, bridge removed. Dew Construction. Millennium Project 1999-2001. New bridge.
Lock 7W Mottram Road Lock:	Concrete cap. Dew Construction. Millennium Project. 1999-2001. Part repaired, part new lock.
Hartshead Power Station:	Canal infilled for 400m. Morrison Construction for Tameside Council. DLG. 1996.
Lock 8W Staley Hall Lock:	Buried. HCS (R) for Tameside Council. DLG. 1996.
Grove Road Bridge:	Piped culvert, swing bridge removed. Morrison Construction for Tameside Council. DLG 1996. New bridge.
Lock 9W:	Cascaded. TCL/HCS (R) 1987/8.
Lock 10W:	Cascaded. TCL/HCS (R) 1987/8.
Lock 11W:	Concrete cap. TCL/HCS (R) 1987/8.
Scout Tunnel:	Portals bricked up. BW. Millennium Project. 2000. Minor repairs.

MOSSLEY

Scout Tunnel – Lock 12W:	Canal channel distorted by slippage of adjacent disused railway embankment. HCS (R) for Tameside Council. DLG 1996.
Lock 12W Whitehead's First Lock:	Cascaded. HCS (R) for Tameside Council DLG 1996.
Lock 13W:	Cascaded. HCS (R). 1990/91.
Lock 14W:	Cascaded. HCS (R). 1990/91.
Lock 15W Roaches Lock:	Cascaded & water level footbridge across lock. HCS (R). 1988-90. New footbridge.

Lock 16W: Cascaded. HCS (R). 1988/89.
Lock 17W: Cascaded. HCS (R). 1988-90.
Royal George Aqueduct: Intact. BW. Millennium Project 2000. New concrete channel.

GREENFIELD
Lock 18W Keith Jackson Lock: Cascaded (1975). Oldham Council/HCS (R) 1988-1990.
Lock 19W Royal George Lock: Cascaded (1975).Oldham Council/HCS (R) 1988-1990.
Manns Wharf Bridge: Piped culvert, bridge removed. J. Fisk & Co. for Oldham Council. DLG 1994-1995.
                                   New bridge.
Frenches Bridge: Piped culvert, bridge removed. Casey's for Oldham Council. DLG. 1995/6. New bridge.
Lock 20W Hall Lock: Cascaded. HCS (R). 1990.

UPPERMILL
High Street Bridge: Piped culvert, bridge part demolished and buried. DCT Constn. Millennium Project.
                                   2000/01. Original bridge rebuilt with new extension.
Lock 21W Wade Lock: Concrete cap. DCT Constn. Millennium Project. 2000/01.
Lock 22W Dungebooth Lock: Cascaded.(i) HCS Volunteers. 1981-1983. (ii) HCS (R). Millennium Project. 1999.
Lock 23W Lime Kiln Lock: Cascaded.(i) HCS Volunteers 1981-1983. (ii) HCS (R). Millennium Project. 1999.
Saddleworth (Old Sag) Aqueduct: Intact. BW. Millennium Project 1999. New concrete channel.

DOBCROSS
Wool Road embankment: 200m of canal infilled. Ruttle Plant Hire for GMC. 1986. New canal channel.
Wool Road Bridge: Piped culvert, no bridge at realigned main road. Original bridge infilled on minor road.
                                   DCT Constn. Millennium Project. 1999-2000. New main road bridge; minor road
                                   bridge excavated and repaired.
(Diggle Lock Flight. Nos. 24W-32W)
Lock 24W Wool Road Lock: Concrete cap. DCT Constn. Millennium Project. 1999-2000.
Lock 25W: Cascaded, part demolished. HCS (R) for Oldham Council. DLG. 1994-1996.
Lock 26W: Cascaded, part demolished. HCS (R) for Oldham Council. DLG. 1994-1996.
Lock 27W: Cascaded, part demolished. HCS (R) for Oldham Council. DLG. 1994-1996.
Lock 28W: Cascaded. HCS (R) for Oldham Council. DLG. 1994-1996.
Lock 29W: Cascaded. HCS (R) for Oldham Council. DLG. 1994-1996.
Lock 30W: Cascaded, part demolished. HCS (R) for Oldham Council. DLG. 1994-1996.

DIGGLE
Lock 31W Geoffrey Dickens Lock: Cascaded, part demolished. HCS Volunteers. 1985-1995.
Lock 32W Summit Lock: Cascaded, part demolished. HCS Volunteers. 1985-1995.
Standedge Tunnel: Major and minor unstable areas, roof collapse near Marsden end. AMCO. Millennium
                                   Project. 1999-2001. (ERDF and Sports Council grants for survey.)

MARSDEN
(Marsden Lock Flight, or Francis Locks – Nos 42E-34E)
Lock 42E: Cascaded, part demolished. Kirklees/West Yorks Councils. 1984.
Lock 41E: Cascaded, part demolished. Kirklees/West Yorks Councils. 1985.
Lock 40E: Cascaded, part demolished. Kirklees/West Yorks Councils. 1985.
Lock 39E. Warehouse Hill Lock: Concrete cap. Kirklees/West Yorks Councils. 1984.
Lock 38E: Cascaded, part demolished. Kirklees/West Yorks Councils. 1985/6.
Lock 37E: Cascaded, part demolished. Kirklees/West Yorks Councils. 1985/6.
Lock 36E: Concrete cap. Kirklees/West Yorks Councils. 1985/6.
Lock 35E: Cascaded, part demolished. Kirklees/West Yorks Councils. 1985/6.
Lock 34E: Concrete cap. Kirklees/West Yorks Councils. 1985/6.
Lock 33E Sparth Lock: Cascaded. Kirklees/West Yorks Councils. 1985/6.
Lock 32E Pig Tail Lock: Cascaded. Kirklees/West Yorks Councils. 1985/6.
Lock 31E Booth Lock: Concrete cap. Kirklees Council. 1987.
Lock 30E: Cascaded, part demolished. Kirklees Council. 1987.
Lock 29E: Cascaded. Kirklees Council. 1986.
Lock 28E: Concrete cap. Kirklees Council. 1987.
Lock 27E: Cascaded, part demolished. Kirklees Council. 1987.
Lock 26E: Cascaded, part demolished. Kirklees Council. 1987.
Lock 25E Shaw Carr Wood Lock: Cascaded, part demolished. Kirklees Council. 1987.

SLAITHWAITE
Lock 24E Shuttle Lock: Concrete cap. Locktail bridge extended over lock chamber. HCS R). DLG. 1994-1996.
                                   Rebuilt with guillotine tail gate.
Lock 23E Dartmouth Lock: Concrete cap. HCS (R) for Kirklees Council. DLG. 1994/5.
Slaithwaite Town Centre: Canal filled in and water piped for 650m. Galliford (Northern). Millennium Project.
                                   1999-2001.

Britannia Road Bridge:	Piped culvert. Bridge removed. New bridge deck. Deck of new road lowered.
Grassed area with cherry trees and car park:	Canal infilled. New canal channel.
Lock 22E Pickle Lock:	Infilled in car park. Lock excavated and repaired.
Grassed area with footpath:	Canal infilled. New canal channel.
New Lock 21E:	New lock above bridge.
Platt Lane Bridge:	Former swing bridge removed, piped culvert. New fixed bridge.
Lock 21E Waterside Lock:	Intact, filled with debris. Abandoned to allow canal to be taken at lower level through new bridge.
Lock 20E Spot Lock:	Cascaded, part demolished. Kirklees Council. 1988.

LINTHWAITE

Lees Mill Bridge:	Access road 1m above water level. Wrekin Construction. Millennium Project 2000. New bridge.
Lock 19E Holme Lock:	Cascaded, part demolished. Kirklees Council. 1988.
Lock 18E. Can Lock:	Cascaded, part demolished. Kirklees Council. 1988.
Lock 17E Westwood Locks:	Cascaded. Kirklees Council. 1988.
Lock 16E Westwood Locks:	Concrete cap. Kirklees Council. 1990.

GOLCAR

Lock 15E Golcar Brook Lock:	Cascaded, part demolished. Kirklees Council. 1990.
Lock 14E Ramsden Locks:	Concrete cap. Kirklees Council. 1989.
Lock 13E Ramsden Locks:	Cascaded, part demolished. Kirklees Council. 1990.
Golcar Swing Bridge:	Fixed in closed position. Wrekin Constn. Millennium Project 2000. New fixed bridge.
Golcar Aqueduct:	Intact. Wrekin Constn. Millennium Project 2000. Concrete channel.
Lock 12E. Rough Holme Lock:	Concrete cap. Kirklees Council. 1989.

MILNSBRIDGE
Milnsbridge Lock Flight (11E-7E)

Lock 11E:	Cascaded. Kirklees Council. 1990.
Lock 10E:	Cascaded. Kirklees Council. 1990.
Whiteley Street Bridge:	Widened, prop in canal. Kirklees Council. Rebuilt, prop removed. 1991.
Lock 9E:	Cascaded, part demolished. Kirklees Council. 1990.
Lock 8E:	Concrete cap. Kirklees Council. 1990.
Lock 7E:	Concrete cap. Kirklees Council. 1990.
Lock 6E Mark Bottom Lock:	Cascaded, part demolished. Kirklees Council. 1991.
Stoney Battery Bridge:	Piped culvert, bridge removed. Wrekin Constn. Millennium Project. 2000. New bridge.
Lock 5E Paddock Foot Lock:	Concrete cap. Kirklees Council. 1991.
Lock 4E Longroyd Bridge Lock:	Intact. Derelict. Kirklees Council. 1991.

HUDDERSFIELD

Haigh & Co.:	Canal infilled for 50m. New channel as part of adjoining DIY store. DLG. 1995.
New Lock 3E:	Costains. Millennium Project. 2000/01. New lock.
Sellers Engineers:	Canal infilled for 300m, factory building. Costains. Millennium Project. 2000/01. New tunnel.
Lock 3E:	Intact, infilled. Costains. Millennium Project. 2000/01. Lock abandoned.
New Lock 2E:	Costains. Millennium Project. 2000/01. New lock.
Bates & Co.:	Canal infilled for 100m, works yard and factory building. Costains. Millennium Project. 2000/01. New tunnel.
Queen Street South Bridge:	Intact. Costains. Millennium Project. 2000/01. Bridge underpinned to allow for new lower water level and low level steel piled channel to old lock 2E.
Lock 2E:	Intact, Derelict. Abandoned.
Lock 1E Stanley Dawson Lock:	Intact, derelict. HCS (R) for Kirklees Council. DLG. 1993.

HUDDERSFIELD BROAD CANAL

University Causeway:	Piped culvert through steel piled causeway. Morrison Constn. for University of Huddersfield. DLG. 1994. New footbridge and sewer under canal.
Wakefield Road Bridge:	Piped culvert, bridge removed. Streeters (Northern) Ltd for West Yorkshire County Council. 1986. New bridge.

NOTES:	(i) TCL = Tameside Canals Limited.
	DLG = Derelict Land Grant.
	HCS (R) = HCS Restoration Limited.
	ERDF = European Regional Development Fund grant.
	HCS = Huddersfield Canal Society.
	(ii) Lock names have previously been published with varying degrees of authenticity based mainly on an 1825 Map by G.Bradshaw, local usage or the inventiveness of the writer. Hopefully the ones here are correct or appropriate.

Appendix 2
Restoring the Canal – Cast of Players

THE VOLUNTEERS

It is impossible to single out those volunteers most responsible for the restoration of the canal from the many active members of the Huddersfield Canal Society involved not just in physical restoration, attending meetings, writing letters and reports, or lobbying for support, but also in running events and festivals, and the many boat crew members. Simple lists can, however, be produced showing who held particular roles.

The Committee of Huddersfield Canal Society (1974-1980) and the Council of Management of Huddersfield Canal Society Ltd (1980-2001):

Brian Beagley:	1974-1978	Vice Chairman (Also Chairman, Peak Forest Canal Society).
Susan Bradbury:	1983-1987	Treasurer.
Margaret Bradnum:	1974-1975	
Allen Brett:	1986–current	(Also Chairman, Rochdale Canal Trust.)
Dennis Broadbent:	1976-1977	
Clodagh Brown:	1978-1979	
Jean Buckley:	1980-1987	Sales Officer.
David Bullock:	1977	Editor *Pennine Link*.
David Calverley:	1992-1995	East Side Chairman.
Gordon Calverley:	1993-1995	East Side Chairman.
Phillip Calverley:	1982	Publications Officer.
Jack Carr:	1985-current	West side Chairman, Chairman Promotions Group.
Colin Chadwick:	1977-1983	West side Chairman, Exhibitions Officer.
Suzanne Chadwick: (ex-Gibson)	1981-1992	Editor *Pennine Link*, Membership Liaison Officer.
Diane Charlesworth:	1977-1981	Editor *Pennine Link*.
Robert Dewey:	1974-1988	General Secretary.
Valerie Dewey:	1975-1976	Membership Secretary.
Trevor Ellis:	1978-current	Vice Chairman.
Christopher Farrar:	1978-1981	Chairman 1979–1981.
David Finnis:	1976-84, 1988-1996, 2000-current	Working Party Organiser, Treasurer, Publicity Officer, Public Relations Officer, Press Officer.
Peter Freeman:	1976-1981	Social Secretary, West side Chairman, Vice Chairman.
John Fryer:	1979-current	Company Secretary.
Keith Gibson:	1982-current	Projects Officer, Chairman Construction Group, Chairman HCS Restoration Ltd (Also Chairman, Northern Canals Association.).
Kenneth Goodwin:	1986-1994	(Also Chairman, Inland Waterways Association.).
Gerry Greenwood:	1974-1977	Editor *Pennine Link*.
Jean Greenwood:	1975-1976	
Christopher Griffiths:	1975-1977	Publicity Officer.
David Irving:	1985-1986	Plant Manager.
Robert Keaveney:	1974-1975	
Neville Kenyon:	2000-current	
Allan Knott:	2001-current	West Side Boats Co-ordinator.
Robert Lear:	1974 1976	
Graham Maskell:	1979-1985	Uppermill Project Manager.
Hazel Maskell:	1983-1984	Festivals Officer.
Robert Maycock:	1992-1995	Boats Officer.
John Maynard:	1974-1986	Chairman 1974-1979, Boats Officer.
David Milsom:	1978-1980	East Side Chairman.
Brian Minor:	1986-current	Festivals Officer, Chairman Promotions Group, Editor *Pennine Link*.
John Morley:	1985-1988	East Side Chairman, Boats Officer.
Timothy Noakes:	1974-1977	
Keith Noble:	1998-current	(Also Secretary, Calder Navigation Society).
Alwyn Ogborn:	1987-current	Editor *Pennine Link*, Special Events Co-ordinator, Chairman Promotions Group.
Garth Pratt:	1986-1992	
Gay Quilter:	1992-1998	Sales Officer.
Alec Ramsden:	1985-current	Press Officer.
Robert Reed:	2001-current	East Side Boats Co-ordinator.
Patricia Riley:	1996-1998	Sales Officer.

Peter Scott:	1986-1988	
Margaret Sinfield:	1974-1975	
Ian Stott:	1978-1979	Working Party Organiser.
John Sully:	1986-current	Treasurer.
David Sumner:	1978-current	Vice Chairman, Uppermill Project Officer, Chairman 1981-current, Chairman HCS Training Limited.
Fiona Tewson : (née Minor)	1987-1994	Sales Officer.
David Wakefield:	1984-1990	Publicity Officer, Editor *Pennine Link*.
Derek Walker:	1975-1978	
Alan West:	1974-1976	
Robert Wilkinson:	1974-1977	Treasurer.
Vincent Willey:	1995-current	Boats Officer.
Stewart Wilson:	1976-1978	Sales Officer, Publicity Officer.
Leslie Winnard:	1977-1983, 1987-1992.	Treasurer.
Kenneth Wright:	1992-current	Vice Chairman HCS Restoration Limited, Editor *Pennine Link*.
Josephine Young:	1992-current	Membership Secretary, Chairman Promotions Group.

The Board of Directors of Tameside Canals Ltd. and HCS Restoration Ltd:

Susan Bradbury:	1985-1987	Treasurer.
David Brown:	1985	
Eric Crosland:	1991-2001	
Trevor Ellis:	1990-2001	
John Fryer:	1985-2001	Company Secretary.
Keith Gibson:	1985-2001	Chairman 1992-2001.
Kenneth Goodwin:	1990-1994	
Neville Kenyon:	1990-2001	
Guy Martin:	1985-2001	
Robert Maycock:	1990-1995	
Brian Minor:	1985-2001	
Keith Noble:	1992-2001	
Frank Ruffley:	1985-2001	Chairman 1984-1992.
John Sully:	1992-2001	Treasurer.
David Sumner:	1985-2001	
Alex Thomson:	1990-2001	
Stephen Whitby:	1989-1999	Managing Director.
Vincent Willey:	1986-2001	
Leslie Winnard:	1987-1992	Treasurer.
Kenneth Wright:	1991-2001.	Vice Chairman 1993-2001.

Chairs of the Tameside Canals Festival:

Peter Freeman	1978
David Sumner	1979
Elizabeth Hodgson	1980
Colin Chadwick	1981
Laurence Sullivan	1982
Vincent Willey	1983
Ken Baker	1984
Brian Minor	1985
Brian Minor	1986
Vincent Willey	1987
Trevor Harvey	1988
Trevor Harvey	1989
Hazel Maskell	1990
Vincent Willey	1991
Vincent Willey	1992
Alwyn Ogborn	1993
Alwyn Ogborn	1994
Tony Wolstenholme	1995
Tony Wolstenholme	1996
Peter Hawly	1997
Tony Wolstenholme	1998
Brian Minor	1999
Shirley Rowbottom	2000
Shirley Rowbottom	2001

The Society employed staff, either directly or by its subsidiary company, Tameside Canals, or HCS Restoration. It is not possible to name them all, but certain key members spring to mind – Stephen Whitby (Managing Director), John McLouglin (Manager,) Ken Dyball (Manager, HCS Training Ltd), Malcolm Braddock (Foreman) Andy Sharpe (Mason), and in the office Frank Smith (General Secretary), Bob Gough and Paula McLoughlin, who were the first point of call to many members of the Society. Only Frank Smith and Bob Gough remain today. And, difficult to categorise, Mike Thompson, the Society's Planning (and all other things) consultant. Not staff, as he often refused payment provided his expenses were met, and not a volunteer as he could not be persuaded to join the Council of Management.

THE OFFICIALS
Members of the Board of Directors of the Huddersfield Canal Company Ltd:

Councillor Riaz Ahmed (Oldham):	1997-1998
Derek Cochrane (British Waterways):	1997-2002
Jeffrey Duffy (British Waterways):	1997-2002
Councillor Eleanor Ritchie (Oldham):	2000-2002
Councillor James Greenwood (Oldham):	1997-2000
Keith Gibson (HCS):	1997-2002
Councillor Brian Mather (Oldham):	2000-2002
Councillor Roy Oldham (Tameside):	1997-2002
Councillor Cyril Pearce (Kirklees):	1997-2000
Councillor David Ridgeway (Kirklees):	2000-2002
Councillor George Speight (Kirklees):	1997-2002
David Sumner (HCS): 1997-2002	
Councillor James Sutcliffe (Oldham):	1997-2000
Councillor Kevin Welsh (Tameside):	1997-2002

BRITISH WATERWAYS
The Chief Executives: Brian Dice and Dave Fletcher.
The Regional Bosses: David Pyrah (Principal Engineer, North), John Freeman (Area Engineer), Stuart Sim.
(Area Engineer, then Regional Manager), Derek Cochrane (Regional Manager, then Regional Director).
And Alex Thomson (Manager, Special Employment Schemes).

THE PLANNERS
John Billington (Oldham), Steve Hughes (Tameside), and John Miller (Kirklees) with Nick Andrews, Graham Birch and John Rooney (Oldham). In addition – not a planner, but responsible for the Derelict Land Grant programme in Kirklees – Geoff Farnell, the Council's Chief Landscape Architect.

THE ENGINEERS
Shalim Chaudary (Kirklees), John Hallam (BW), Joanna Heap (Oldham), Lee Holland (Tameside), John O'Kelly (BW), Neil Maxwell (BW), Michael Marshall (BW), Neil Morton (Wilde & Partners), Graham Pointon (Oldham), Peter Rawson (Tameside), Freda Rashdi (Oldham), Tom Rowe (BW), Ian Selby (BW), Malcolm Stakes (BW), Alan Stopher (Hudds. Canal Co.) Colin Thompson (BW), Mike Thompson (Oldham), Jon Walsh (Kirklees), Andy Wheeler (Kirklees).

THE COUNCILLORS
It's almost as difficult to single out key members of the councils as to pick out key volunteers, but, I think this is a fair list of those most influential:
Allen Brett (GMC), Geoffrey Brierley (Tameside), John Crowther (Oldham), James Greenwood (Oldham), George Hatton (Tameside), Dorothy Lindley (Kirklees), Alan McFadyen (Oldham), Roy Oldham (Tameside), Cyril Pearce (Kirklees), Garth Pratt (West Yorkshire), Leslie Preece (Kirklees), Peter Scott (GMC), George Speight (Kirklees), John Sully (West Yorkshire), James Sutcliffe (Oldham), Kevin Welsh (Tameside).

Sources & Bibliography

BIBLIOGRAPHY

Bairstow, Martin, *The Leeds, Huddersfield & Manchester Railway; The Standedge Line*, (Bairstow, Pudsey, West Yorkshire, 1984).

Bolton, David, *Race Against Time*, (Methuen, 1990). ISBN 0 7493 0994 6

Brook, Roy, *The Story of Huddersfield*, (Macgibbon & Kee, 1968).

Brown, Geoff, *The Black Flood - What caused it?* (Saddleworth Historical Society Bulletin, Volume 18, Number 2, Summer 1988).

Brown, Geoff, *In search of the Standedge Admiral*, (Saddleworth Historical Society Bulletin, Volume 21, Number 4, Winter 1991).

Burnett, John, *A History of the Cost of Living*, (Pelican, 1969).

Burton, Anthony, *The Great Days of the Canals*, (David & Charles, 1989; re-printed Tiger Books International, 1995). ISBN 1 85501 695 8

Burton, Anthony & Pratt, Derek, *The Anatomy of Canals - The Early Years*, (Tempus, 2001). ISBN 0 7524 2137 9

Chadderton, David, *The Diversion of The Huddersfield Narrow Canal at Diggle*, (Saddleworth Historical Society Bulletin, Volume 4, Number 4, Winter 1974).

Calder Navigation Society, *West Yorkshire Waterway Guide*, (Calder Navigation Society, Fifth Edition, 1992). ISBN 0 9512400 13

Chadwick, S. *All Stations to Manchester*, (Huddersfield, 1949).

Charlesworth, Diane, ed., *The Huddersfield Canals Towpath Guide*, (Huddersfield Canal Society, 1981)

Crump, W.B. *Huddersfield Highways Down the Ages*, (Huddersfield, 1949).

Fox, Michael, *Woolroad and The Huddersfield Canal*, (Saddleworth Historical Society Bulletin, Volume 17, Number 3, Autumn 1987).

Fox, Michael & Peter, *Pennine Passage: A History of the Huddersfield Narrow Canal*, (Huddersfield Canal Society, 1989). ISBN 0 9514270 0 8

Hadfield, Charles & Biddle, Gordon, *The Canals of North West England*, (David & Charles; two volumes, 1970).

Hadfield, Charles, *The Canals of Yorkshire and North East England*, (David & Charles; two volumes, 1972 & 1973).

Haigh, E.A. Hilary, ed., *Huddersfield: A Most Handsome Town. Aspects of the History and Culture of a West Yorkshire Town*, (Kirklees Cultural Services, 1992). ISBN 0 900746 51 3

Handford, Michael, *Huddersfield Perspectives*, (Article in IWA "Waterways" Journal, April 1983).

Haynes, Ian, *Stalybridge Cotton Mills*, (Neil Richardson, 1990). ISBN 1 85216 054 3

Haynes, Ian, *Mossley Cotton Mills*, (Neil Richardson, 1996). ISBN 1 85216 109 4

Hill, Samuel, *Bygone Stalybridge*, (1907. Reprinted MTD Rigg Publications, 1987).

Holt, Alfred, *The Story of Mossley*, (Mossley Civic Society, 1974; reprinted and revised, 2000).

Hunt, J.M. *John Rooth & Co., Carriers on The Huddersfield Canal*, (Saddleworth Historical Society Bulletin, Volume 11, Number 1, Spring 1981)

Jenkins, D.T. *The West Riding Wool Textile Industry 1770 - 1835. A study of Fixed Capital Formation*, (Pasold Research Fund, 1975). ISBN 0 903859 05 X

Keevill, Graham, *Standedge Guide; an Industrial Landscape of Roads, Canals and Railways*, (Kirklees MC, 1986). ISBN 0 9511224 0 1

Kirk, Neville, *The growth of Working Class Reformism in mid Victorian England*, (Croom Helm, 1985). ISBN 0 7099 1551 1

Kirklees Metropolitan Council, *Huddersfield Narrow Canal Information Pack*, (Kirklees MC, 1984). ISBN 0 900746 15 7

Laybourne, Keith, *Britain on the Breadline - A Social and Political History of Britain between the Wars*, (Alan Sutton, 1990). ISBN 0-86299-490-X

Lock, Alice, ed., *Looking back at Stalybridge*, (Tameside MBC, 1989).

Lockwood, Ernest, *Colne Valley Folk: The Romance and Enterprise of a Textile Stronghold*, (Heath Cranton, 1936).

Lower, John, *The South Pennine Ring*, (The Hallamshire Press, 1998). ISBN 1 874718 37 7

Lucas, Mike, *I'd go back tomorrow*, (Wayzgoose, 2001). ISBN 0 907864 88 0

Owen, David, *Canals to Manchester*, (Manchester University Press, 1977; reprinted, 1987). ISBN 0 7190 2631 8

Ransom, P.J.G. *The Archaeology of Canals*, (World's Work, 1979).

Rolt, L.T.C. *Narrow Boat*, (Eyre & Spottiswoode, 1944; reprinted Budding Books, 1998). ISBN 1 84015 0645

Russell, Ronald, *Lost Canals and Waterways of Britain*, (Sphere Books, 1982).

Schofield, R.B. *Benjamin Outram 1764 - 1805. An Engineering Biography*, (Merton Priory Press, 2000). ISBN 898937 42 7

Singleton, Fred, *Industrial Revolution in Yorkshire*, (Dalesman Publishing, 1970).

Smith, W. John, *Saddleworth Buildings*, (Saddleworth Historical Society, 1987). ISBN 0 904982 06 8

Strong, Roy, *The Story of Britain. A People's History*, (Pimlico, 1998). ISBN 0 7126 6546 3

Worker's Educational Association, *The Saddleworth Story. Historical Essays by students of the Saddleworth Branch of the Worker's Educational Association*, (WEA, 1964).

Wyles, David, *The Buildings of Huddersfield: Four Architectural Walks*, (Kirklees MC, no date given). ISBN 0 900746 16 5

OTHER SOURCES

1. Canal Company Records. Huddersfield, Stalybridge and Oldham libraries each have two full microfilms of the original Huddersfield Canal Co. records, consisting of: Minutes of the General Assembly of Proprietors of the Company, Minutes of the Committee, Share Books and Annual Reports for the years 1794 to 1845.

2. Minutes of the Committee of the Huddersfield Canal Society, Council of Management of Huddersfield Canal Society Ltd and of the Boards of Directors of its subsidiary companies, and of the Tameside Canals Development Association.

3. Files of the Huddersfield Canal Society and its subsidiary companies.

4. *Pennine Link*, the journal of the Huddersfield Canal Society.

5. Newspaper cuttings.

6. Reports as follows:

The Report of engineer Benjamin Outram, of Butterley Hall, in the County of Derby, on the Proposed Canal, from Sir John Ramsden's Canal, at Huddersfield, in the County of York, to join the Canal at Ashton-under-Lyne, in the County of Lancaster. Huddersfield, 22 October 1793.

The Report of the Survey of the Huddersfield Canal by Robert Whitworth (Snr). Letter to the Proprietors of the Huddersfield Canal dated 11 August 1797.

An abstract of the Report of Mr Thomas Telford, engineer, relative to the state of the works on the Huddersfield Canal, from an actual survey. In pursuance of a Resolution made at a meeting of the proprietors of the said canal. 24 January 1806.

The Facts About the Waterways, British Waterways Board, 1965.

The Huddersfield Narrow Canal – a Unique Waterway, Huddersfield Canal Society, 1975.

A New Canal for Huddersfield, Huddersfield Canal Society, 1976.

Huddersfield Narrow Canal Recreational Survey. Kirklees Metropolitan Council, 1977.

Through Stalybridge by Boat, Huddersfield Canal Society, 1977.

Fill't to't top wi' rubble – A Community View of the Huddersfield Narrow Canal in Mossley, Huddersfield Canal Society, 1978.

The Canal in Uppermill. Action! – For Restoration, Huddersfield Canal Society and Saddleworth Historical Society, 1979.

Inland Waterways, Arteries for Employment and Spending, Inland Waterways Amenity Advisory Council, 1980.

Economic Benefits of Cruising Waterways - a study of boaters expenditure on the Stratford-On-Avon Canal (North), British Waterways Board Recreation Planning Research Paper, 1980.

'A Report on the Job Creation Potential of the Huddersfield Narrow Canal as a Navigable Waterway.' Huddersfield Canal Society, 1982.

'A Proposal for the Restoration of the Huddersfield Narrow Canal from Marsden to Slaithwaite.' Huddersfield Canal Society in association with Colne Valley Society, Marsden Community Association, Slaithwaite and District Angling Club, and Pennine Heritage, 1982.

'Proposed Restoration of the Huddersfield Narrow Canal from Ashton to Stalybridge'. Huddersfield Canal Society and Waterway Recovery Group, 1983.

'The Huddersfield Narrow Canal: No longer a derelict eyesore through Tameside'. A report on the restoration of the canal by a Community Programme scheme between Division Bridge and Mottram Road. Huddersfield Canal Society 1983.

'The Huddersfield Narrow Canal – the brief for a Cost Benefit Study'. Huddersfield Canal Society and W.S. Atkins & Partners, 1984

'Huddersfield Narrow Canal: The Benefits of Restoration'. L&R Leisure Consultants in association with PIEDA Ltd, 1986

'Potential Access related projects in the Tame Valley'. Tameside Canals Ltd. 1988

'UK 2000 Projects: Huddersfield Narrow Canal. Towpath Restoration within the Metropolitan Borough of Oldham', The Civic Trust, 1989

'Huddersfield Narrow Canal; Standedge Tunnel Condition Study',Ove Arup & Partners, 1989

'The Standedge Experience', L&R Leisure PLC in association with Derrick, Wade & Waters, First Interpreters, and Transport for Leisure, 1989

'Completing the Restoration of the Huddersfield Narrow Canal – A Bid for Resources', Huddersfield Narrow Canal Joint Committee 1993

'A Study to Assess the Impact of the Restoration of the Huddersfield Narrow Canal', Coopers & Lybrand, 1994

'Completing the Restoration of the Huddersfield Narrow Canal – Strategic Programme of Reclamation', Huddersfield Narrow Canal Joint Committee, 1994

'The Huddersfield Narrow Canal; A demand analysis for boating and informal recreation activities on the re-opening of the navigation', British Waterways Marketing Research Unit, 1995

'Completing the Restoration of the Huddersfield Narrow Canal – Strategic Programme of Reclamation', Huddersfield Narrow Canal Joint Committee, 1995

'Huddersfield Narrow Canal Environmental Heritage Audit', Civic Trust, 1996

'Completing the Pennine Ring – A Millennium Project', Huddersfield Narrow Canal Joint Committee, 1996

'The Standedge Experience; Proposed Visitor Centre: Tunnel End', Marsden Brooke Millar Peden Architects, 1996

'Completing the Pennine Ring. The Huddersfield Narrow Canal Millennium Project Business Plan', PIEDA plc, 1996

'The Standedge Experience Marketing Strategy', British Waterways, 1998

'The Standedge Experience: Feasibility Study', Sykes Leisure, 1998

'Standedge Visitor and Information Centre – Modified Option 2', British Waterways, 1998

'Waterways for Tomorrow', Department of the Environment, Transport and the Regions Policy Paper, June 2000.

Index